STONY HARRIS

YOUNG DUMB & FOOLISH

Authorunit
17130 Van Buren Blvd., Ste. 238,
Riverside, CA 92504
877-826-5888
www.authorunit.com

ISBN 979-8-89030-339-4 (Paperback)
ISBN 979-8-89030-340-0 (Ebook)

Printed in the United States of America

Contents

Introduction

Paul & Peter was identify twins but they didn't know it. Their mother had to give them up. For adopted when they was infant because she got sick she couldn't care for them no longer. She thought because they was brothers they would keep them to together. But little she know they was separate. And they grow up different Paul adopted parents give him the best. And send him to collage he became a lawyer. Now he own two law firm.

Peter parents didn't money. They have much but give him a lot of love. And they taught him if he work hard he can become whatever he wanted to be. As long he keep God first in his life. They keep him in church also.

But the twins didn't know there was attended the same church East Baptist.

One Sunday I (Freedom) decided to go to church alone. And she saw Peter in church. Because he was well dress thinking he got bank (rich).

And she was tired taking care dead beat guys. And they wanted her act like their mother. Now she looking for someone taking care of her for a change. Let see did she find that man of my dream.

Dedication

I wanted to thank God
for allow me to put this book together.
And my lovely wife Dorist L. Harris.
Who stood by my side?
And friends and family.
I pray you would enjoy this book.
Please share it with others.
And thank you for all your support.

Chapter 1

Are You For Real?

Girl, you got to meet this man that I saw at church this morning. He so fine then wine and well dress. Please come church with me this Sunday. I just know he got bank (money). Maybe he have a friend rich too.

What you mean? Penny look up. Hey, I'm isn't into all that. I just want a simple man to love me unconditional.

Charity suffereth long, [and] is kind; charity envieth not; charity vaunteth not itself, is not puffed up.

Child, please I got to mine. I want to living in a big white house on the hill. Ride in the best car money can buy. Especially get my wig done every week. And go shopping whenever I want too. Spare no money. Eat in the best restaurant every night.

Freedom you must be crazy. And out of your mind thinking you isn't going to work for it.

Now days you don't know what you might have to do for it. Casting down imaginations, and every high thing that exalteth itself against the knowledge of God,

And bringing into captivity every thought to the obedience of Christ;

Well, I'm just tired of take care a dead these beat men. I want someone take care of me for a change.

I do understand where you coming from.

But, I know you must be dreaming. Thinking you going find a man like that.

Penny don't hate girl. It someone out there for you too.

Every time I want to do something special for a change. Like for an example go to the movie and get something to eat. My ex always looking in my pocket. Hoping I'm going to pay for it. Or he come up with an excuses I forgot my wallet at home.

Girl, I just pay my child support. You know I love you go ahead pay for this time. I got it the next time. It make me feel like I'm his mother. I'm isn't trying to take care no one child. I had to do that with my sister and brother.

Mom had to work I'm was the second oldest girl.

When my oldest sister turn 18 she ran away with her boyfriend. And she end up got pregnant. And I was stuck at home. Then I told myself I'm tired of this life. One night I saw this movie. This prince found his queen and take care of her for the rest of her life.

Why this can be me someday?

Hey, don't be jealous it enough rich man go around. Freedom smile.

Girl, I told you once! I'm not jealous. What you mean?

Some man want you change your lifestyle for them.

And that isn't me. I will change when I'm ready. I won't allow someone trying force me too.

That why I don't go church anymore. Because the Saints try to change me. But mom made us go with her every Tuesday, Friday night and Sunday anyway. When I was young.

Yeah, I remembered those day too.

I and my sister, brother use to start crying. Hoping mom change her mind let us stay home with dad.

But it didn't work. She told us we going to serves the Lord in her house. Freedom with a serious look on her face.

And if it seem evil unto you serve the LORD, choose you this day whom ye will serve; whether the gods which your fathers served that were on the other side flood, or the gods of the Amorites, in whose land ye dwell: but as for me and my house, we will serve the LORD.

Or go find you again place to stay.

And we wasn't going to hang out with these devils. And bring in bad spirit.

I had to laugh. That the first time I heard that. Freedom shake her head.

That wasn't funny we couldn't play with our friends. Only at school and after church while mom walking around talking to everyone.

Sorry, Penny but your mother sound like she didn't play. No! When it comes down to the Lord.

Oh, I never forget when the Pastor one Friday night preaching about demonic spirits.

That man sacred me so bad I almost pee in my clothes. What happen? I look up at her.

For they are the spirits of devils, working miracles, which, go forth unto the kings of the earth and of the whole world, to gather them to battle of that great day of God Almighty.

A lady woman yelling. Oh Lord their here. The hold church scream.

At the same time it was lighting and thunder that night too. The light started blanking off and on. I fell to my knees I crawled under the pews went to the bathroom. Sweat was running down my face. And my heart was pouring so fast. I just barely made to it.

Since that night I play sick mom let me stay home with my dad. It been over ten years ago.

But I still read my bible sometimes and watch the gospel station on television every Sunday morning.

Well, I got think about it.

Okay, Penny but I hope you do it for me. Because you owe me a favor anyway.

Oh, you going there.

Girl, I thought I pay you back. No!

Well, I got go find me a perfect dress. And buy a new wig too. You know I got look good for my man.

Girl, you is crazy.

Because you know we don't suppose to be out here looking for a man. And you want me go with you to church.

Yes, yes, I heard that all my life. And mom say that it in the bible.

Yea, I know it somewhere in the book of Proverbs.

Whoso findeth a wife findeth a good thing, and obtaineth favour of the Lord.

But, but if I wait too long some else might grab him before me.

Then I be looking foolish seeing another woman driving my car. And wearing my clothes, wigs.

Oh, I can't forget my 3in. pump.

That probably give me a nightmare. I don't need that. Freedom, Freedom!

What?

I think you already having a bad dream. Girl, you need go get some help.

I think you have too much water on your brain. Whatever you been drinking please stop.

Na, since you went there with the bible. It also said God will supply all my need. And said if I ask he going give me desires of heart.

Delight thyself also the Lord; trust also in him; and he shall bring it to pass.

Yep, that true.

And I (Freedom) believe it too. Because I ask him give me that man in my name.

You better go back read the whole chapter again. So you can get the right understand it.

Penny, don't worry I know what I'm doing.

Yes, that what wrong with some people thinking that way. And make a big mess then they be looking foolish. How you know if he don't already have a family. Or he could be a killer?

Don't get your heart broken by your foolishness thinking. Wise (men) layup knowledge: but the mouth of the foolish (Is) near destruction.

Girl, I told you already I can handle myself. Na, that isn't going to happen.

And everyone that hearth these sayings of mine, and doeth them not, shall be likened unto a foolish man, which built his upon the sand:

Okay, whatever!

Hey Freedom, you got go now.

Some of us got to work around here. I got to pay some bills. I'm isn't trying be homeless. And I need to do something with this hair. Penny grab a brush.

Yep, I know that right. I'm tired looking at your wig all over your head anyway.

Oh, no you didn't go there. You don't have to be jealous because this all my hair.

What about yours? Freedom.

Aw, aw some of this is my hair. But I bought the rest. I know my man going to like it. And that what matter. Plus you didn't cook

Freedom! What?

My name isn't Jesus.

Yes, I know he feed ten thousand people. But you won't feed me.

But Jesus said unto them, they need not depart; give ye them to eat. And they say unto him, We have here but five loaves, and two fish. He said, Bring them hither to me. And he commanded the multitude to sit down on the grass, and took the loaves, and the two fishes, and looking up to heaven, he blessed, and brake, and gave the loaves to his disciples, and the disciples to the multitude. And they did all eat, and were filled: and they took up the fragnment that remained twelve baskets full.

And he give them a bag take with them too.

But you didn't bring nothing in. So why you think you should take something out. Penny you didn't go there.

Beside I haven't been grocery shopping yet. It take money which I don't have right now.

But I can give you a cold glass of water. So you won't get thirty while walk down to the bus stop.

Yeah! I hope you have a good night.

Now, I know I got go catch this bus. Before I be your roommate tonight.

Na, I think I hear the bus coming around the corner. So you run out there jump on it.

I love living alone. I'm like my dad. He don't mind let someone stay over. But he going let you know Jesus arose in three days. Don't get comfort. Because you got to leave in three days. He think all grown people should have their own place. Or have a place to go.

I know your daddy lost his mine.

Chapter 2

It's Doesn't Make Sense

Girl you know I love you. I see you tomorrow. Yep, Penny he just like you lost your mind.

Okay, you don't have put me out. I just leave.

And I thought you're my friend with a sad look on her face. What you mean? I'm your friend.

You didn't feed me.

Girl, I told you haven't went shopping yet. But you can give some money help me.

Penny, if had some money I won't need to eat over here.

Well, let me stop by mom house before I go to home. I know I can always get a hot meal there. Because I know dad don't miss a meal. He getting bigger than his car. Before he know it he going to need a school bus. Mom always warned him said she going buy him a king size bed. Because a queen isn't bigger enough.

Okay, so why you worry me?

I finally made to mom house.

I run up on the porch getting ready knock on the door.

That old dog jump out the window. He sacred me so bad I jump back off the porch and started screaming.

Dad run out the door with a bat in his hand.

Girl, you almost got your head knock out. And you know old Joe (dog) if he hear any noise going attack. I told you need call us first. If you going to come over here this late.

He already got the mailman wearing his running shoes. Now he just throw our mail on the porch. And he yell you got mail.

While he running back to his mail truck.

Come in, why you over here this late? I'm going let you know don't ask for no money. Because we have it.

Mom walk in the living room.

Hello, darling why you over here this late. Is something wrong?

Woman, you late I just that question already. Na, I was over Penny house. She didn't cook.

When do she ever cook?

Daddy, she do cook. But she said haven't been grocery shopping yet.

I heard that before.

Hey, did she had some bread?

No! If that case I would have made me a sandwich. And I went on to the house. I wouldn't be over here begging you for some bread.

Wow, Freedom that too bad because she could held up the bread. And pray just like Jesus did, she may had two loaves of bread and two baskets of fish.

Daddy, you trying be funny.

So, I stop see If can get a hot meal for the night. Girl, I thought I taught you how to cook.

Yes, ma you did.

But I don't have no food in my house. I had too many bills late month.

Yes, right if you stop spending all your money on that old fake hair. And getting your nail done. You would have some food in your house. And you don't have come over eat up my food up. You know we don't get pay once a month.

And you know they don't want give us some food stamps. But they always want to get into your business. Asking you hundred thousand question. And they already knowing they are going to turn you down. Talking about you make too much money. I had to tell this fool. If

I make too much money I wouldn't be down here standing this long line begging too.

I have been young, and now am old; yet have I not seen the righteous forsaken, nor his seed begging bread.

Mom, you going let dad talk about me like that?

Well, he may have a good point there. Because every time I see you look different.

Mom, I got look my best I'm trying catch me a rich man. Then I won't have to eat up your food dad.

Girl, what you been smoking or bump your head on something. That will never happen. I wish you wake up out that dream.

Dad, you just jealous because mom isn't rich. Girl, who are you talking to this way?

I think you better change that attitude. Before I change it for you.

Sorry, dad.

Mom, I find a man he got bank (money). What you mean?

He got money.

Oh, yes where you meet this man? Young girl,

Daddy I was at church.

Okay, but you better careful these men. What you mean? Mom

Because some men come to the church. Prey on young girls like you trying got a play.

Well, yea of course they going dress well. And call their self a saint of God. Until they get you in their bed. Then it be a total different story. Or get you pregnant.

Because look at your daddy I thought he had some money too. When I find out he didn't nothing but some old clothes. He was sleep in his car.

That what mess up my head up. He was house sitting for a friend house. And wearing his clothes and driving his car too. I thought it was his house.

By that it was too late I already married him and was pregnant with your sister.

Mom, tried to warn me. And she told me if I married this man don't come back home crying. Because you're making a mistake and she was right. I been living with this nightmare for years.

I thought he would be dead by now. I even buy some extra burden insurance. So I be alright when he gone. But I think God punished me.

Why?

Because he still breathing and won't stop bought me. Because I didn't listening.

Daddy, why you lie to mother.

Little girl, first of all I didn't lie to your mother. Because she didn't ask the right questions.

So I didn't tell her. But she could left long time ago.

I wish she stop blaming me for something she wanted to do anyway.

That what wrong some people in a relationship or married. What you mean Dad?

Girl sit over there so maybe you won't end up like your mother. Okay!

What I'm try to say when you find out that person isn't right for you. Or you don't have anything in comment. Why stay with them. When you can walk away from it. But some don't won't leave. Because they try make it work out.

But one thing forget if God don't approved it. It won't work. Then again some may not know that God must be a part of it. Be honest that what happen to me and your mother. We both went in this relationship blinded.

What you mean?

At first there wasn't no God in it.

I look over at her. She drop her head knowing I was telling the truth.

Because I wasn't going church at the time. Until I met your mother.

And I heard some people say they will make it work out. Whatever it take.

In the back of my mind I want to yell fool you can't change no one if they don't want. Only you can change yourself.

Let no man deceive himself if any man among you thinks that he is this age, he must become foolish, so that so that he may become wise.

People use all type of excuses to stay in it. Even through some getting abuse. They say it love if my man or woman isn't hit them. Or they yelled at them. That isn't the way God want us live your life.

Okay, Dad think I hear the bus coming around the corner. Thanks for your advice.

Girl, I don't hear nothing. You just want me to shut-up. Na, isn't like that. You know I love you.

But I got to go home. And I got up early for work. Or I can stop working come back live with you guys again.

Nope, that isn't going to happen. I made your room a junk room. What you mean? A junk room you making sure no one come back.

Yep that right. That the hold idea eating up my food. You using my light and hot water. If you don't know that got to be paid. You already know you and your brother hate pay bills.

Na, Dad I pay my bills.

Yep, if you don't want be homeless.

I guess so.

But I still hear you complaining about you don't have no money anymore.

Dad, I can't help it. I got other things to buy too. Like my wigs and get my nails done. Dad you know these guys isn't going to look my way. If I look like plain Jane they something caught their eyes.

What? Girl I know you gone crazy.

No, dad you wouldn't look at mom if she didn't look her best. But if a woman have long hair, it is a glory to her: for her hair is given her for a covering.

Aw, aw!

I can't hear you. And why you clear your throat now.

Girl, go home before you get me into trouble with your mom. You don't have to live with her.

Let us this conversation alone.

You sure be graceful you have a place to stay. And you pay on your bills.

I see these young people don't know how value a dollar. But I thank God for mom teaching spent our money wise.

Some of us don't get their money once a month. After pay the bills sometimes they barely have money for food.

Sorry, Dad you right. I see you later.

Hey, mother I forget my plate. I'm isn't on a diet or fasting. Girl, you need too. It won't hurt you trim down just little bit. I told you better get a part time job.

I don't need it when I drop by here time to time grab me a plate from you guys.

Girl, get out before I baptism you in the Jesus. Bye, mom.

Dad putting me out. I love you.

Don't pay your dad any attend. He just saying he love you in his our language.

Yep, you know he fell on his head one to many.

I see you women always sticking together around here. A man can't win a fight.

Yea, Dad you can't but you just have to love us. The both burst out laugh.

I finally got my plate and ran to the bus stop.

Hoping this bus haven't left me already. If so I matter well get ready walk home. I should've got my plate and left.

No, I had mess with dad.

Well, let sit down take this load off my feet.

I heard a loud music. I look up it was the guy. I saw at church. I want him to be my man.

Hey, he have a woman in his car.

I drop my head I should have ran up to him. Introduce myself. Before I left church. I guess I was too exited lost my mind

Maybe, I could have be riding with him. Instead of me out here trying catch this bus.

But I got to find away get her out of my car.

I know, I'm going to be there in church get some more details. Before I make my move.

Now, I got fight for my man. I better roll up my sleeves and put on my dancing shoes.

But little she knew, she saw the wrong brother. It was Paul with his baby sister on their way home.

Hey, girl wake up! Guess what I saw last night while was on my way home?

I don't know, and right now I don't care. I'm trying sleep you know I got to get up in an hour for work.

Ok, Penny you don't have to be mad at me. I will talk you later.

Oh, sorry girl let me get up. Lately I been towing and turning trying make myself go to sleep.

Okay, you just need a man touch that all.

Na, isn't that I been working late. Trying get this money. Because I don't have a man.

Girl, soon I get my man. I will see if he have someone for you. Hey, would do me a big favor? Freedom

Okay, what?

Shut up you just like me. You don't have a man either.

So why you sitting yourself up? I don't want you hurt yourself. Na, isn't going to happen.

And what you mean? I might hurt myself.

Some of us don't realize people don't always hurt. We hurt ourselves by wanting something so bad. And we won't accept no.

This I say then, Walk in the Spirit, and ye shall not fulfil the lust of the flesh.

For the flesh lusteth against the Spirit, and the flesh: and these are contrary the one to the other: so that ye cannot do the things that ye would.

Yea, yea but that isn't me. I told you once I can handle myself.

Okay, have it your way.

I will keep a towel close. You just might need it.

Girl, I know why I call you now. Guess who I saw last night? While I was on my way home.

Who?

My man, he was with a woman in my car. Now you already know what I must do.

If I run up on her anywhere. I'm going grab that old wig off her head. And I'm going to drag her down to the river.

Why?

Because I'm going to baptism her in the father, the Son and the Holy Ghost.

When come up out of the water she going to speaking in tongue four different language. For trying take my man.

Girl, you sound like your grandma. Yeah!

She didn't mine fight for what she wanted. Poor Mrs. Bee God bless her soul.

Wait a minute Freedom! What?

You don't own a hub cap and talking about you have a car. Plus you can't ride a bicycle. I know no one better not give you any license. I'm going to call my family and friends.

Why?

So they can move out your way. They may get ran over. Or get someone kill.

Plus you can't die yet because you still owe me.

Please pay me soon. I can use that cash to help buy me some new mattresses.

Which it long overdue for some new one. Maybe I can throw this old pads away. Because it making my back hurt. Sometimes I have roll out the bed. To make my back to get act right.

Please leave that a lone.

You know I don't like funeral. Watching people sitting up in church crying and falling out. Because they feeling guilt. They didn't call that person.

Or stop by their house to see if they help.

Some make up excuses like they was tried because they always work. Or had other things to do more important. And they didn't have transportation to get there. But if it was the other way round they would be upset. And they would start bad mouth.

Lord, they will be the first one confess they are a Christian.

When you lookup they talk about that person so bad. Like there isn't no God in them.

Yeah, I heard that too.

Thou hypocrite, first cast out beam out of thine own eye; and then shalt thou see clearly to cast out the mote out of thy brother's eye.

No, I can't do that isn't in my nature. I am not going to fight for a man.

Plus that might be his wife. And if do get close to him. He just might not won't you. Here you are wasting your time. When you could have waiting on God. Give you the right man.

But let patience have her perfect work, that ye may be perfect and entire. Wanting nothing.

Oh, Penny he going to want me. I know how make him love me. Girl, your head just like a rock. My mom use to tell me this all the time. When I growing up.

What you mean?

No one can't tell you nothing your mind up. Yeah!

For if a man think himself to be something, when he is nothing, he deceiveth himself.

Wait a minute, I told you once that I pray when I first saw him be mine under my breath. And that he have a fat bank account. Lord, removed this stumble block out my way.

See girl, got to have faith.

I know I read that somewhere in the bible one night. No faith, no man.

But without faith it is impossible to please him: for he that cometh to God must believe that he is, and them that diligently seek him.

Yeah, that true too. But it also say.

Let no man deceive himself if any man among you think that he is wise in this age, he must become foolish, so that he may become wise.

Hey, I need you come with me tomorrow Freedom.

Girl, I can't do that I got to work. I need my j. o. b.

After tomorrow you don't need it. Because I going to sign you up for a crazy check. They going to give a stray jacket and a shoot in your behind to come you down.

Well, let me get off this phone. So I get ready for work I will talk you later.

Chapter 3

It Time To Make That Move

Good morning Freedom, I see you come in a good mood. You must had good weekend.

Oh, hello Mrs. Well yes I did I saw my man yesterday at church. Hold up, you got a man! How you got a man? All the men I saw you with you leave them. Because you said they didn't have no money or they won't work.

You know what the bible say if a man don't work. He can't eat. For even when we were with you, this we commanded you, that if any would not work, neither should he eat.

That right, that why I had to let them go. I refuse take care another man again. When I know he can do it his self. But this one have banks.

What you mean? He own a bank.

No, Mrs. Well it mean he already have money.

Girl, you know you can't be using these big words around me. When you talking to me I'm old school.

I like my words plain and simple.

Let me told you about my Grandson.

I and Greg was on our way to the store one Thursday night.

He yell Grandma! I say what baby.

Did you that bad whip (car) pass by us?

I shake my head I look up in the mirror at him. I said boy before knew it.

What you talking about?

And he say that bad car Grandma. Okay, what wrong with the car.

He burst out laughing.

No, no nothing wrong with their car.

It have a beautiful paint job, nice rim and tires on it.

Lord, these kids will mess up your mind. The things they say now days.

Yeah!

Hey, we better clock in before we be later. Okay, Mrs. Well.

Boy, I'm tired of this old place. They want you work like a slavery up in here. Plus it hot too. And in the winter it be too cold you got keep on a big coat on trying keep warm.

Some of these women don't know the meaning of washing their self. And brush their teeth. They always want to be in your face laughing and talking to you.

Yeah, I know someday I look up ask God why me? I have to smell this place. I can't wait to go home. When I hit the front door.

I be yelling free at last. I know those people think I'm crazy. Yeah, I'm just little touch.

Yes, you're Freedom. We burst out laughing.

But they don't want pay us what we worth. Yes, I know that right Freedom.

I been here so long I just pray for more strength just make it through the day.

Yes, it was hard at first when my kids was younger. Coming in here. Trying put food on the table and keep a roof over our head. That why I know there is a God watching over me. I call him Jehovah jireh he my provider.

But my God shall supply all your need according to his riches in glory.

Now I'm old no one won't me now but God. Because of my age so I guess I stick around here. Help these young people out.

Thinking they know everything but they don't know nothing. Plus I need this old insurance here. You know I'm isn't young anymore.

Okay, I understand Mrs. Well.

I got go to my machine get her start it up. I don't need the boss standing over me.

Bye, I see you at lunch my friends.

I went on to my machine. Wishing I wasn't here.

Good morning, Mrs. Jolly how was your weekend?

Girl, it was great after had a fight with the devil first. (My husband) I have to tell you all about at lunch time.

Because we don't have time right now.

Okay, I throw my hand in the air.

I better text Penny at lunch remind her I want her go to church Sunday with me.

Oh, I think I will go to bible study Wednesday night. Maybe I can catch my man there. Let him know he going be my man. Na, that don't sound right. It sound like I'm demanding him what he going to do.

Some men don't like a woman telling them what to do. Because they like to control the situation.

But I would have you know, that the head of every man is Christ; and the head of the woman {is} the man; and head of Christ {is} God.

I better back that thing up before I push him away.

Lord, I got find another way get his attended.

Well, I can fall out in front of him. But he just might not pay me any attend and walk out the door. Or yell for the ushers come and get me. That won't work.

Hey, Freedom are you still having those dream again? I shake my head look up to see who calling my name. It Mrs. Dean the boss wife with her hand on her hip.

My eyes got big and my heart started pumping fast. Knowing I'm in trouble.

Yes Ma,

You know we are paying you to work not staring into space. And you better watch your hands before you accidently put them in that machine.

Think it a piece of wood you going come back with no hands. And remembered we isn't going to pay you a dime. When it your fault. But I will call 911 come and get you. Because I don't want your blood all over my machine. And I got pay someone to stay over to cleaned it. I'm isn't trying do that. We need cut to down on the cost anyway. We paying you girls too much already for nothing.

Now, you have a good day. And if I catch you again just standing there doing nothing. I will give your last pay check.

Wow, that woman don't play. Freedom you better watch yourself. Before you having your last meal here.

Mrs. Conner yell across the floor. Yes Ma, I will.

I wondered what Mr. Woody did to this woman make her so cold heart. She are lucky wasn't talking these young girl.

They would've whip her behind long time ago. And they won't care about their job.

Yea, now that be funny maybe she will treat us much nicer.

I would love take that picture. Hang up it by my machine. I bet we wouldn't have to worry about her coming back on the floor no more. Talking crazy to us.

The both burst out laughing.

Boy that was so close. I better run into the restroom to wash my face get my head together.

I know, I better get this man looking my way. So I can get out this place.

No more work for me.

I ease out of the restroom hoping I don't have any more problem with this woman.

Hey, Freedom, how was your weekend? Oh, it was lovely I think I find my soul mate.

Freedom look back as she walking back to her machine.

Oh yea, you must tell me all about it later. How you find him. Maybe I will find my too.

This old man I got he too old fashion. He don't know what a woman need.

He want to sit around the house all the time. Now, he won't take me no way anymore.

But that okay. I told him keep sitting there. Looking a big old bull frog. Guess he think I all need a kiss on the cheek. And hear that I love you before I go to work.

That man think I'm a fool. What you mean? Miss. Low

He just love what can I do for him. That why he won't leave.

Oh, a real woman want a man be gentle, sometimes come home say baby I'm going take your load off of you today.

Just sit down let me cook for you for a change.

Oh, bring her some flower and maybe some candy. He don't forget the card. Put the kids in bed turn on some music. Ask her can I have the first dance my love. And you know what happen next.

What Miss. Low?

Just say he put a smile on your face the next morning. Oh, you so nasty.

No, girl that make a woman feel good about their self. Knowing her man showing some love. And I love it too but that haven't happen in years.

That problem why half of time I'm so evil. When I come up in here. Hearing those others woman come in smile and in a good mood on Monday. Talk about how they got their groove on with their man. Here I'm wishing that could have been me.

That why I told him one day I'm going to step out. I'm isn't coming back to that boring home.

I might be getting old. I'm not dead yet. That man going to miss all this beauties. Yep, I heard that. Miss Conner yell.

That sound like me in that same situation. Oh, I didn't thought no one heard me.

Okay, I better get back to work Miss Low. Yep, me too.

I know, I won't have to worry about that my man going blow my mind.

Freedom whispered under her breathe. As she walk back to her machine. Now come on bell I'm getting hungry.

This big girl need to eat don't want pass out. Then someone be running over here trying give me cpr. And they problem need some mouthwash.

Aw, oh no now that would be nasty putting their lip on me.

Now on the other hand Penny slowing walk in the break room. Wishing it was the weekend so could go back to bed.

Hey, Penny with a hole in it. Look like someone in a crappy mood this morning.

Yeah! Sorry I don't mean to look like this. It seem like my weekend cut off short.

Why you say that? Danny look down at her.

Well, my friend Freedom stop by my house last night. And all she want to talk about this man. She never meet only saw him at church. Now she calling him her man. And now she want me go to church with her Sunday. Just try to get close to him.

Well, are you going with her? Man, I don't do church anymore.

But don't get me wrong I do believe in God.

And I love read my bible too. I also pray every day and before I go to bed. I love me some gospel music.

Plus I don't feel right up in there helping her catch this man. Mom, taught us girl you don't have any business looking for a man. But be open if a man want to talk you.

I try to tell my foolish friend you don't suppose do that. And I told her the bible say it the man job look a woman.

Okay, then what say? Danny stood there.

Yes, she think know all that. But she isn't trying hear that. She believe if she don't make the first move on him. Someone else will. And she think he got money too.

Yep, you need to go ahead sign up get a check. She sound she nutty than peanut. Lost her my mind. If a man want her she don't have to worry no one can come between them.

Other word you telling me she don't have no patient. Yeah, Danny you got that right.

Now that can be danger two way?

Oh, what you mean? I got hear that from a man point of view. I just may learn something.

Okay, first of all can get her heart broken. Because in her mind she already picture how this man going to be when she get this man.

Thinking he going treat her like a queen.

But if she don't be careful now day. You don't know what she putting herself in. He could be abuser and jealous. Now that be bad for her health. If he break her will. She will accept anything. Just long she have him beside.

I saw that happen over and over in my family. What!

Yep, my sister (Eve) fall in love with this married man. Thinking he was going to leave his wife for her.

Now, that was a lie. Okay, what happen?

He had a good job and a nice car.

They met at bar.

Couple of her friends beg her she need get out of the house more often. But she always turn them down.

So one night she gave in finally she said yes.

But she wasn't going to drink anything. Just relax and try enjoy the music.

Let me make this story short. She met this man that what her friend told us. He keep on buying her pepsi cola. We thought it wasn't any harm. Think it was cute a man was interesting in her. Because she haven't a man since her baby daddy left. For another woman that been over 5 year ago.

Little we knew it was spike with liquid. She got so drunk she couldn't stand up.

And they had to carry her out to the car. And carry her up a thousand stairs put her to bed.

Somehow he slip his number in purse.

One day she was looking for something in her purse. She found this number it the guy who got her drunk.

I still ask myself why she had to call that man. Eve wasn't the same.

Why you say that? Penny cross her legs?

She found out the man was married and have kids. But that didn't stop her.

She still wanted to be with him. And she start sleeping with him.

Nevertheless, to avoid fornication, let every man have his own wife, and let every woman have her own husband.

And you already know what happen next. She got pregnant now she really thought he loved her enough to leave his wife. Because they going have a baby together.

Hey, did he leave his wife?

Yea, right no he told her she better get rid of the baby. And he gave her the money to do it.

Because he wasn't going to leave his wife. She was taking of him.

Eve break down in tears. And she didn't know why someone would do her so wrong? She was confuse this man said he loved her. Soon she told him she was pargnant thing twist.

Well, what happen did she get rid the baby?

Girl, no mom taught us if we make a mistake deal with it. So Eve remembered that was a commandment.

Thou shalt not kill

Plus the child was an innocent soul. But every time she look at her son. It remembered her what she done.

And now she regretting the fact she didn't listening to other. Try to tell her leave that man alone move on.

But every man is tempted, when he is drawn away of his own lust, and enticed.

Then when lust hath conceived, it bringeth forth sin: and sin, when it is finished, bringeth forth death.

Wise men layup knowledge: but the mouth of the foolish is near destruction.

Wow, Danny I pray that don't happen to my friend Freedom.

Well, I better go with her to church with her. I may have pick up the pieces. Even though I don't do church anymore. Because this girl have a strong will whatever she set her mind to do. She going trying it. Now that what I'm afraid of. But she still my crazy friend. I don't understand she told me she saw this man with a woman.

Wow, that sound he got a woman.

Wait minute Danny, but that don't mean that his woman. It could be a family member or friend needed a ride.

That true.

Why do some men think if a woman seem with a man? They sleeping together or in a relationship?

I don't know!

I didn't know we was in a debate Penny.

Yeah, bring it on. I got protect our women right. Okay, you trying get something start here.

I'm ready it my time ask the question Danny set back in this chair.

But remembered all men isn't bad.

Well, that case all women isn't bad just some of them.

Why do some woman think it okay sleeping different partner? So what you call them?

Penny!

Maybe she looking for a man for fill their need. Or for the money.

Boy, that in the bible prostitution.

Also thou shalt not approach unto a woman to uncover her nakedness, as long as she is put apart for her uncleanness. Oh yea, what chapter you found it in?

I don't remember right now. But I will look it tonight bring it to you in the morning?

Okay, I want to read all about it.

Now my time Penny look at him. Hit me with it.

Why do they call some men dog?

Well, that easy some men like sleep around with different women.

But I'm isn't the one. I think that so nasty to much stuff out there. And some thing you can't get rid of it. You got live with it.

Now we better cut this conversation short.

And get some work done. Before we both be standing in line ask some government cheese.

Okay, okay Penny. You start it.

Yeah I did now I'm going end it.

I got get paid. Penny look up at the clock. Hoping it close to lunch time.

I have a bad feeling what Danny said about his sister. Freedom could be heading in the same direction. Somehow I got to figure out how get her mind out this man. Because who know what kind of man is he. I can't standing round see my friend get hurt over again. So I better roll up my sleeve see what can do.

By that the bell ring.

I jump up grab my lunch and cell phone. Walked fast to the break room.

Hey, Penny, someone must be hungry.

Yes, I am I didn't have time make me some breakfast. Well, what you bring for lunch?

I brought some old tuna sandwich. Boy, I hope you got some breath mint.

I love me some tuna too. I put tomato, pickles on it. Okay!

Penny your phone ringing.

Oh, that would be Freedom. My friend I telling you about. Okay, well I got check in with the wife. I see you back in the office.

Oh okay, Danny I got answered this call anyway.

Chapter 4

You Need A Life

Boy, you have all this money. Why you so alone?

If that was me I have all type women knocking my door down. And I have me a date seven day a week. Rick smiling as sat down across Paul.

Man, I'm isn't like that. Because I have money. I don't want for anything. I can go out on the street find that. But that be nasty and unclean. I want the right woman. Who isn't out for my money? Who going to love me unconditional love. If I lose everything she stand by me whatever happen. She still love me. Charity suffereth long, {and} kind; charity envieth not; charity vaunteth not itself, is not puffed up,

Rick your mind all twist up.

Boy, you better sit your old self down somewhere. And find you a nice woman who going to put up with your mess. Because some of these women will mess up your little world.

It is better to dwell in a corner of the housetop, than with a brawling woman in a wide house.

And you later.

Hey, what you mean? Paul

I already prayer God send me the one.

Now I'm going to sit back and wait on her. In the meanwhile I'm getting myself ready.

Boy, I know you lost something up there.

I hope you find her soon. You better get yourself out there go looking. Before all the good woman be gone.

Na, I'm isn't worry about it. What is mine? It will be there for me?

Rick, I see you don't have no patience nor faith

But let patience have her perfect work, that ye may be perfect and entire, wanting nothing.

And all things, whatsoever ye shall ask in prayer, believing, ye shall receive.

But without faith {it is} impossible to please {him}: for he that cometh to God must believe that he is, and {that} he is a rewarder of them that diligently seek him. Yea, that may be true.

Now, I see you running woman to woman. And you still isn't sanctify.

Yes, I am!

Paul, who you trying fool we been friends ever since we was smaller. You know me and I surely know you.

So stop lying. If that so why have a woman by now? Any way let drop that subject. I need your help.

Really? Yea!

Oh, you need me go on line find you a date. Rick!

What?

Shut up, I'm for real. Let me tell you what need before you answer.

Okay, okay, he burst out laughing.

I have 3 people from my law firm about to retire. And I need someone to replace them soon.

Do you know someone be interest in the job? Now, you can speak or hold your peace. Rick Well, let me see.

Hey, I don't want none of your throw away girlfriends.

I'm looking for someone meek and humble. I don't need a girl come in when she feel like, always running late, loud, always on her phone talking to who know. Or come in wearing too short dresses nor tight clothes. I don't need my guys women all come up here. They want to beat her down. Because she all up in their face smiling. And having police snooping around here. I isn't trying lose my clients. We all work hard to get them. That who paying our bills.

I like things decent in order.

Let all things be done decently and in order.

But I know isn't never be perfect. I'll going to do my best make it safe and clean. Paul smile.

Because I have a lot of faithful people working there. Plus they don't mind roll their sleeves up work over to get the job done. To make the business run smooth.

I promise, I won't let them down.

And they just don't know how much I appreciate their dedication.

So I got to keep them happy. Because of them and without God help this place wouldn't be on the map.

Boy, you always trying go by the good book.

Yeah! Rick that my secret. Putting God first without him this place been fall all apart. And you wouldn't be my right hand man.

You just don't know I pray everyone morning. When I pull up in the parking lot. And before I leave this place. I thanking him for it and the people who run it. Because they depend on this job pay their bills. And keep a roof over their head family. And put food on their table me too. I like said before without them. I'm nothing. So I can't lie like I did it all by myself. Paul shaking his her.

I am the vine, ye are the branches: He that abideth in me, and I in him, the same bringeth forth much fruit: for without me ye can do nothing.

See that what my good book say.

That why so many business closing their doors. For once they don't acknowledge God first.

Thou shalt have n others gods before me.

Wow, brother I didn't know you became a saint.

Well, yes when Daddy die last years. I promise I will get my act together. And I been working on it. I start back going to church. Now I got Don going with me.

That girl went wild after mom die. What you mean?

She started drinking until she pass out front of the kids. Little Tony use to call me tell his mom on the floor. And she won't get up. And having party sending the kids over her neighed house.

And she have bad kids too. She been having different guys over her house all hour of the night. You already know I don't play around my niece and nephews. If any would of happened to one of them. I know I be on my way to jail.

So I had to step in get things righ.

Mom, didn't play that especially when come down to her grandkids.

She was mad at me because I don't have any kids.

But I had to tell her mom I'm isn't ready. Plus I haven't found the right woman yet.

Who want to be a family?

Oh what she said then? Rick smile.

Nothing, but look up side my head. I know wanted to hit me with her bible.

Yea, that sound like her. At first I was scared of her the way she look at me. When I use to come over your house play video games with you back in the days.

Na, she won't harm a fly. But until someone push her to the limited. Then you will have problem.

You already know how John was (BAD). He thought he was grown when turn 12 yrs. old.

Yea, he did.

Let me tell you what happen one day I was with him.

These boys was twice his age mom told he plain and simple don't hanging around them. Because they smell like trouble. So John didn't want hear mom.

One day he was hanging out with the boys. But he didn't know they was selling drugs. A guy name Bug I think he was 16 at that time. He use to keep money. I guess John wanted be like him.

We didn't have money like that. That what we thought. Because mom never told us was rich. I guess she wanted us be a normal person. Or she was afraid we spin out wild. So she keep us humble. And I'm thankful she did.

Humble yourselves therefore under the mighty hand of God, that he may exalt you in due time:

John explain to me. Bug saw the police he ask him keep this bag for him. So John put it in this book bags.

He said okay, he didn't know what was in it.

By that time Bug take off running. But he said he wondering why he left him standing there.

The police turn around and jump out of their cars. Yell get on the ground with your hand behind your back. He hit the ground and when I look up there was five police all around him.

Boy, when mom heard about it.

And she had to go down to the police station to get him. John said he saw mom walking though the double doors.

He yell please let me stay. I already know going to happened to me.

What? The officer look at him.

Because my behind going to be on fire tonight. I just might have to call you guys back put me out.

Mom, going to get me.

The police look at him burst out laughing. Well, I can't help with this one.

Boy, you better watch who you pick to become your friends the next time. Some say they are but they will use you. If you don't be careful. For their personal gained.

Beware of false prophets, which come to you in sheep's clothing, but inwardly they are ravening wolves.

Yup, that my mom John drop his head. And grab his behind.

The phone ring.

Excuses me, I need answered this call.

This my secretary.

Okay, I need to use the restroom anyway.

And I'm getting ready go home Rick throw his hand in the air. Ask he was walking the door.

Hi, Gail what up with you? I know have something good for me.

Oh, I do! I just calling let you know I was look over some applications. I saw one you maybe interest in.

Okay, what he or her name? Oh, it a lady.

And why should I be interesting in her? Oh, her name Penny Louis.

Because she been on this waiting list over 6month. To get in here. Wow, Gail that is a long time.

Okay, let me have her application in the morning.

So I can look over it. I hope she still interesting in the job. Thanks, I see you in the morning.

And have good night.

Okay, same to you Gail getting her thing to go home.

Hey, what are you smiling about? This morning and early too. Paul walked in stood by coffee machine.

Gail tell me this lady put in application 6 mo. Ago. Are you serious?

Yep! Paul. I pray she need a job. Maybe we can use her.

Well, that good news. But I hope isn't a hood rat. I hope isn't ugly and her all over her head.

The both burst out laughing.

Me too I sure don't need that round here.

Now that would be bad business.

Judge not according to the appearance, but judge righteous judgment.

Chapter 5

She Just Don't Know

The phone ring.

I bet this Freedom.

Let me answer this phone I already know what she want. Girl, you know I'm still in bed trying get my beautiful rest. Yes, I know that why I calling you early. So you can look your best. You know what today is?

No! But it not my birthday.

Penny, stop playing get out of the bed.

It Sunday and you promise me you going to church with me this morning.

Na, wait, wait I said I was going to think about it.

Oh, you going to do a sister like this. You know I been there for you. When you ask me go with you to meet this guy. You know he was crazy with all that nasty tattoos all over his body. And he had a Mohawk.

He sure fool you because he use someone else pictures. We both back up when we saw him and ran the over way. Okay, okay, I will go but I'm isn't going seat in the front.

Oh, great I'm already.

So I will meet you there. I will text you the air dress. Let me jump in the shower and throw some clothes on. I talk you later.

Bye, you better not set me up. Girl, I told you I'm come.

Freedom! What?

S. h. o. u. t. u. p! So I can get ready.

Boy, I know God going to get us. This foolish girl going to look for a man at a Church.

Boy, I better be careful.

Before I be wearing a strait jacket too foolish around this crazy girl.

And how I'm let her talk me into going with you. Knowing I don't want to go.

And everyone that heareth these sayings of mine, and doeth them not, shall be likened unto a foolish man, which built his house upon the sand:

Well, I here go. I wondered what should I wear. Because the last time I been there they had plain clothes on.

Oh, I know what I wear that old yellow and black dress. And my black hi.

Hey, freedom I'm on my way. Now I got wait on this slow bus. Okay, I'm be here waiting outside.

I finally made to the church. But once I step off the bus I started feeling funny as I walking around the corner.

I better call this girl make sure I'm going in the right direction. Hey, where you at? Freedom I'm look at a big white church.

Okay, I'm just come around the corner. You will see me in my new dress purple. And gold and my new hair too.

Okay, now I see you. Thanks, you make it.

Well, we better go in get a good seat. Freedom smile and gave a hug.

Okay, as I getting ready walk up the stair. I noticed everyone wearing black and white. And the old ladies looking at us with a funny look on their face.

Hey, Freedom something isn't right.

I think we need turn around go back down these stairs.

Aw, they just ushers they always wearing black and white uniform. You're so right you haven't been to anybody church in a long time. You don't know what is an usher?

Yeah! I can't lie standing in the house the Lord. Penny look up at her.

Girl, we here now. And I hope my man here too.

So I can seat close to him. Maybe I can slide a note with my name and numbers on it

No, Freedom I'm telling you something isn't right. Please come on here let go now.

Hey, here us a good seat. It isn't too close to the front. Nor it isn't too far in the back. It just right.

Penny, stop be afraid something going to happen to you. Just seat down please try enjoyed yourself.

He better be here I waited a hold week just to see him. Freedom looking around.

Wait a minute did you get his name last Sunday? So if you could ask somebody. Instead running around with your head cut off.

Aw, no! I didn't have the time. Plus when I look up he was already gone.

What? Penny jump forget where she was at.

Girl, sit down I'm working on it as you speaking. I know he will be here.

Everyone please stand an old deacon yell.

The door open.

And I peek to see what going. I saw this black car backing up to the door. Two men got out the car they too had on black.

Oh, no she didn't do this to me. This a funeral.

I know, I got run up out of here. Soon they bring in the casket. I'm gone! She can come with me. Or she can stay I don't care.

Please hurry up give me a strait jacket. And give me a shot in my hip put me asleep now.

I think. I losing my mind. This girl got me at funeral. And I don't know anyone here.

I stood up getting ready break out of this church. An usher run over please be seated. And she whisper in my ear the family isn't here yet.

And we need everyone stay in their seated.

I look over at Freedom mad. I just wanted to choke the life out of her.

And hit her in the chest to bring her back to life.

Now, here I'm looking foolish. I matter well cry alone with the family. And play it off. So I can go to the restroom wash my face. Maybe I can slip out the side door.

I look around when I finally found the side door. It was another usher at that door.

I run in the restroom look up. I yell I'm trap.

Boy, I can't wait tell my girls what happen to me. I know they will fall out of their chairs dying laughing at me.

Well, let me go back in take my seat. Try play it maybe it be over soon.

Hey, ma would you like to sing a solo. For the family because the other solo got sick.

Who me?

Yes you will do? The Usher smiling.

Na, thanks! I can't sing Penny whispered.

By that time I open the door getting break out running. my phone rang.

It better not be Freedom looking for me.

Hey, girl I'm going to kill you for bring me to a funeral. And I never seem these people in my life. Plus they had the nerve ask me to sing a solo. And I can't sing.

Hey, I'm isn't that girl you want to kill. Did I call you in a bad timer?

I don't know. If you are a bill collector. Yes!

Hold, on who are you? And who are you looking for? I think you got the wrong number.

I'm looking for Penny Louis.

Well, this is she. Don't ask me for money. Because I don't want to hurt your feeling.

They bursting laughing. Sorry but you too funny.

Miss I'm isn't a bill collector. Nor I'm don't need your money. But who are you then?

Oh, my name Paul. You put in application with us six month ago.

Sorry, but I put in so many application. I can't remembered their names.

Oh, this Donald's law firm.

Now I remembered every time I call you never return my call. Oh, I'm so sorry.

This maybe could be your lucky day.

I'm looking for someone work in the supply room. Because we have some people getting ready to retire. I got to replace them soon.

It pay petty good and come with benefit package. When you been there 60 days.

I hope you available come in for interview Friday even. Paul smile.

Oh, yea please stop playing with me. I know this must be a dream. I'm already at a funeral with my friend. she trick me to come with her. Because she looking a man.

And what more going to happen to me today? And I think you doing the same.

Whoever you are?

Ma, sorry I'm for real. If you don't believe me. Stop by Lee bar q and grill. On 31 and Bullet Ave.

And see for yourself. If I'm playing with your mind. I hope to see you there at 6pm. That give me enough time finished some business up. And run home change my clothes.

Okay, I'm going to take that dinner.

Man, I haven't had bar-q in a long time. And I heard they have great meals. If this meal free. I already told you. I don't have any money. And I'm not trying to wash any dish for this meal. And you better not run out the back door leaving me with the bills.

Oh, you got a deal. Paul got excited. And he burst out laughing. Oh, what so funny?

You! Sorry.

But wait a minute if you try something that I don't approved of. I'm going to hunt you down. And I will became your worthier nightmare.

Hold on miss. I promise I'm be good. Because I love some of me.

Well, see you then.

Wow, this one maybe hard to handle. But I love a challenged. Paul look down at the phone as he sat it down.

I walk out the restroom everyone was leaving.

Hey, Penny where you ran off too? I been looking for you. And see this church is too big for someone get can lost in.

Boy, I been in so many room I thought I was in a maze. Trying find my way home. Ask Freedom trying catching her breathe.

Girl, I went into the restroom. When I seem the casket rolling down the aisle.

You know what I told you. What?

Stop play with me.

Do I have to spell it out?

I don't do church and especially funeral. I don't want to go to my own.

Why I want to go to a funeral someone. I don't even know them or their family. And the usher had the nerve ask my sing a solo.

I'm out here and I won't look back.

Penny, please for forgive me. I didn't know they was having a funeral. My bad.

Did you read the newspaper? No, why?

Because you would knew it. Before you ask me put on my clothes. Come out here.

And I hope, I don't have a nightmare.

I'm done with you. I'm going home to calm down. Hope you found what you looking for.

Don't call me for any more with your foolishness. I could been in my bed making sweet love to my bed. While I watching my Sunday gospel station. Getting my praise on.

No, I didn't see him. Freedom drop her head. Maybe we can come back next Sunday.

Girl, don't even think about ask me. You already know my answered.

No! No! I won't coming back. Because I know what the good book say. About looking for a man.

If you want to do it. That on you my friend. But I won't be a part of it.

Why you won't give it up? And go sit yourself down somewhere. W.a.i.t. on God.

Girl, you know God is too slow for me. I think I will help myself. Maybe I happy be once again.

And be bills free because he going take care for me.

Okay, Freedom you acting like my mom use to call us. When we didn't listening to her.

What?

Your head just like a rock can't tell you nothing.

For if a man think himself to be something, when he is nothing, he deceiveth himself."

Because you think you can do it yourself.

Isn't nothing wrong with my head? I told you don't be jealous.

Hey, when I got home. I'm going to throw my clothes out of my closet. I'm going to jump in to pray for you. For you have a change your mine.

But thou, when thou prayest, enter into thy closet, and when thou hast thy door, pray to the Father which is in secret, and Father which seeth in secret; shall reward thee openly.

Yeah, I need to do the same come on my man. I need you now. Girl, stop been funny.

But when ye pray, use not vain repetitions, as the heathen do: for they think that they shall be heard for their much speaking.

Chapter 6

How Amazing You Are

I got home lay cross the bed I couldn't believe what happen to me today.

Let me find me something to eat. Then I will jump in the shower maybe I start feeling better.

I got to leave this girl along. She isn't right bright in the head. As, I getting out the shower the phone rang.

I jump out the tub grab the towel. And ran over grab the phone to answer it.

But was too later.

I look down at it was mom calling.

Why mom calling me this late?

I hope something isn't wrong with dad.

I better call her back.

My heart start pumping fast. Hey, mom what going on?

What you mean?

Can a mother call their daughter sometimes to see how they doing?

Yes ma, sorry I thought something wrong with you or dad.

I'm fine and your old daddy still alive. I wish he would go ahead die. So I could use the burden insurance money. But he won't die and I can't kill him. They might find out I done it. And lock me up. I just need a long vacation away from this man.

Why mom? What dad did now?

Penny, darling he always wake up complaining about something.

The house isn't clean, or the way I cooking.

But I do clean up the house. I always cook the same way for years.

I think your dad losing his mind. What you mean?

Because he will sit in his rocking chair when he eating he drop crumbs all over the floor. And leave his plates or his drinking glass all-round the house. And he think I suppose go behind pick them up.

Wow mom! Dad trying turn you into his maid. Yeah, but isn't going to happen.

Girl let me tell you what happen Saturday morning. I got up early cook some breakfast. I had the house smell so good with eggs and bacon.

Your daddy walk in the kitchen look around. And he did say good morning.

I started making his plate. And he look up side my head. He said to me he isn't hungry. Put it in the garage can.

Boy, I was so mad at this man. You could have seem smoke from my noise. I took that food gave it to the dog. And I didn't cook any more that day.

Later he came back in the kitchen yell where the bacon and the eggs.

I told him ask your best friend.

Woman, stop play with me you I'm hungry now. I'm ready to eat.

And no I don't have any friend.

Yes, you do that old dog looking up at you. See him smiling at you.

Because he ate your breakfast.

Woman, no you didn't give him my food.

Yeah! Why he licking his paws he just finished.

Hey, I married you not that dog. And whatever I tell you supposedly do it.

You say what Mr.?

Woman you better read your bible again. Now who you talking to like this?

Yes, I am your wife. You keep running your lips you going wake up one morning a lonely man.

Okay, let see what it said.

But I would have you know, that the head of every man is Christ; and the head is the woman is the man; and the head of Christ is God.

See woman I was right. Now go in that kitchen cook me some to eat.

Hold on I isn't going to cook you nothing.

Because God know you was wrong the way you talked to me. Now, if you hungry I think you better get off your big butt. And go into the kitchen if you something to eat.

I'm going watch some news now. And when you finished wash whatever you mess up. Don't disturb me.

Mom, I hope I don't end up with a man like dad. He too much for me.

Oh, what happen did dad cook? Penny smile.

Yeah, but he was mad. He didn't speak to me all day. And I was so glad because I had peace in the house for a change. And I slept like a baby.

Oh, sorry how are you doing?

I just had to tell you how your dad been acting. Maybe he need a crazy shot.

What?

You know what I'm trying to say. Just something to claim him down.

Mom, please stop dad going to be alright.

Oh, I know when I go call the doctor. And let them pull down his pant. And hit your daddy in hip with this needle. I won't have to worry about him at least 6 month.

Girl, what we going to do with him?

You already know how your daddy so stubborn. And stuck in his ways.

Only way he going to change. If God his self-come from heaven. Tap him on his shoulder tell him. If I can't find your name in the book of life. You already know where you going to join your friends in the lake of fire.

Mom, just call Aunt Bib and her posse the old ladies from the church. Stop by the house catch dad taking a nap. And then pour their Holy oil all over him. And fall down on their knees pray. And see the demon rise up. And leave him.

When they finished with him he be speaking nine different tongues.

And when the day of Pentecost was fully come, they were all with one accord in one place.

And suddenly there came a sound from heaven as of a rushing mighty wind, and it filled all the house where they were sitting. And the appeared unto them cloven tongues like as of fire, and it sat upon each of them.

And they were all filled with the Holy Ghost, and began to speak with other tongues, as the Spirit gave them utterance.

Yeah, I like see that day when that happen.

Or if I can carry him down to the nursing home with him other friends. He will just fine.

Mom, I think Freedom need to go too. Why? What she done now?

I think you better sit down.

This girl running behind this man thinking he got money. Hoping he will take care of her.

Now, that funny.

Hold on let me turn off the television. I got hear this.

Mom, she said she saw him at church about two week ago. Okay, so what the problem?

She don't know his name or speak to him.

So she talked me go to church with her this morning. You already know I don't do church anymore.

But I went anyway when I got there. I knew something wasn't wrong. When I saw the people in black and white.

Hey, that sound like they was having a funeral.

Yeah, mom they was and my foolish self-sitting there.

Mad I didn't know no one or who die. And I couldn't leave until it was over. Because the usher standing in front of the doors.

And they had the nerve ask me sing a solo. What?

Yep!

Now that was awful. Making my baby sit though it. Mom, started laughing.

Sorry, I couldn't help myself.

This girl got up went look for this man. But he wasn't there. Mom, I wanted to kill her. But I had to remember she still my friend. And someone got look out for her. Because she nutty and some need help.

Hey, can your keep a secret Penny? Yes, why?

Don't tell nobody because they going think you lost your mind too.

Okay, mom I better go now. And get ready for bed. I got to go work in the morning.

Or you make dad clean out my old room. I can always come back home.

Girl, now I know you lost your mind. Thinking your father going allow you to come back.

The answer is big no.

That the reason your dad did it. To keep the kids out of his house. You know what he going to yell. If you grown it time get your own place.

And please don't look back. He going to you give your clothes and a bible. As you going out the door he going look you in your eyes. And say if you need anything don't call him. Just ask God he will take care all your needs.

Ask, and it shall be given you; seek, ye. Shall find; knock, and it shall be opened unto you: For every one that asketh reveiveth; and to him that knocketh it shall be opened'.

Dad isn't right that man need two check. Because is the one crazy. But I got love he is my daddy.

Mom, I will talk you later. Okay, baby I love you.

Wow, mom must be lonely. I'm going to buy her a good book. Maybe she won't be bored.

Let me get in the bed and I hope this phone don't ring anymore most tonight.

Chapter 7

I Had A Dream

Hey, man! Yes, what up?

I need you house watch for me. You say what?

Peter, I got go out the county for a month.

Because my parents need me handle some business.

While I'm there.

Okay, but I need your car keys too. Why? Doug look up at him.

So I can find me a woman. I'm tired been alone. You already know these women today. They don't want a broke man doug grab suitcase from the closet.

I'm just average man with a 9 to 5 job. Live in my parent old house.

My car barely running but thank God for it.

Look at you can have almost any woman you want. Because you have to money.

I wish, I had it like you. I won't have to worry about my light get cut off. Or food in the house.

See some people just bless like that born into money.

And some grew up poor. They didn't know where their next meal coming from. Pete drop his head.

Boy, please you just don't know sometimes I wish I didn't money.

Because when I was younger mom didn't allow me be a kid. I couldn't go out alone with my friend. I always had someone looking over my shoulder. And I about better not do any things wrong. They will tell it before I got home. I finally found a girl wanted hang out with me. It was hard to be alone.

She always ask me why we couldn't be alone.

I just made up something like my daddy is a police. And he don't trust no one. So he hired someone keep an eyes on his family while gone out town.

I couldn't tell her the truth my parent had money. Because she problem went back tell everyone.

Something could happen to me or some of my family members. I started hating my life.

Why? You have everything you wanted. Man, yes but I couldn't a normal kids.

Like you was Peter.

Man, what you called normal? When you step out your front door sacred you may get catch up in a drive by shooting.

Or see your family member or your friends get gun down. In front of you and started thinking it could be me maybe next. Because now you're a witness. And you don't have nowhere to hide. Because everyone in the neighborhood know you or your family.

And you afraid leave your house. You be thinking a drug addict going you to break in your house take your things.

Sell it for drug. And some don't care if you was there or gone. Wow man! I didn't don't know. I couldn't handle that one.

Yeah, but I didn't have any choice. I pray each day that my parents would move out this neighborhood.

I couldn't go to public school.

Some of those private school teacher is so nasty.

And some think they talk to you any kind of way. I seem it all some of my friends. Especially if you a boy you will get punish for no reason.

If the teacher don't like you. Or they find out who their parent was. If they didn't like them. And they knew if you tell your parents they wouldn't believe you. Because you a little kid. And they will lie their way out it.

I remembered my teacher when a new girl come in. He will spend a lot time with them. If you know what I mean.

That why a lot girls parents take them out school. Because they say they being touch. Some teacher try black mail. If you don't sleep with them. Some underage girl end up pregnant by their teacher. And the school will denied it to protect the teacher right.

Now, that why some of these kids isn't right bright in his head today. And they gone into depression or kill their selves.

Because they are tired of the nightmare.

What they had to go though as a kid. When they didn't have no one protect them.

Wow, that crazy Peter drop his head. Now, see money isn't everything.

For the love of money is the root of all evil: which while some coveted after, they have erred from the faith, and pierced themselves through with many sorrows.

Yes, you right but I can't find a woman isn't all about the money. Now that why I'm in this big house alone.

What? Doug, I think you lost your mind.

Yeah, let me lose my mind. I wanted someone love me. And I want to settle down be a family man. Try to enjoyed one another.

Boy, you better go to the church get you a holy woman.

Who that say they love God.

That where I'm going Sunday morning with a smile on my face. I know she is waiting on me. I'm going to looking and be ready.

Now I think you crazy Peter.

No, I isn't because the bible say if a man findeth a woman. And obtaineth favour of the Lord.

I know that will be me someday.

Yea, yea my uncle Rob you use to say that all the time. To my sister Melody. But she always look up at him funny.

And she whispered over to me say he don't know what he talking about.

I'm isn't thinking about boys right now. Because the boys at my school they always act nasty and calling me bad name.

Uncle must been drinking again.

I better go now I got to go work in the morning. I'm isn't like you don't have to work. If choose too.

Now that isn't true my parents made me work. When I was younger I had feed the horses. And washing all the cars after school.

They thought it will keep my mind off girls. But they didn't know I wanted to run away.

Okay, I will babysitting the house for you. On one condition I want permission to step in your world.

While you out of town. I always wanted to know how to feel being rich. Peter smiling.

Okay, now we have a deal.

Oh, I need some spending money too.

Hey, wait a minute Peter you trying to rob me.

Now good bye I see you Friday night. Before you think of something else you.

Hey, look around my house. I want to come back the house the same way I left it. Doug shake his hand.

Oh, don't worry I will be here with a smile on my face. Doug we been friend a long time. And I hope we can still be friend. When I come back.

Boy, I am going have some fun now. I know I will find that woman. Peter whispered under his breathe.

Oh, first of all I'm going try out the churches. I know a lot of single women going to be there. So I will throw on one of Doug suit, shoes, maybe one of his gold watches. And I have the keys to the cars too.

Boy, I can't wait the girls going jumping all over me. They going thinking I'm rich.

Boy, I owe Penny a big apologize. I should I have check things out. Before I ran out here wild. Now that was a selfish move of me.

Looknot every man on his own things, but every man also on the things of others.

So I better call her to see if we still friend. On my lunch break. Because she haven't speak to me or called. In a week now. I won't do that again.

Hey, why you over there talking to yourself Freedom Miss. Joan peek around the corner.

Oh, this past weekend I just made a fool out of myself.

Now I can't wait until the bell ring. Why?

Girl, you got tell me all about it. You know l love juicy news that my middle name.

Juicy!

You too funny.

My weekend was a nightmare. Why?

My sister came over act like she didn't know where the door was. And she didn't come alone.

What you mean?

Girl, she brought her twin's boys. I call them Cane and Abel.

They tow up my house. And they ate all my foods up too. I wasn't going grocery shopping until the next weekend. Now I don't have a choice or go hungry.

My old man was so mad. When he came home from work that night saw the house. My man told me if this happen again. I'm going have to sleep in a motel for that night.

And I had other plains but it wasn't babysitting her.

And her bad children.

Boy, I think I would went crazy up in there too. But I would have to find away get them up out my house.

See you did it the nice way. If that was me I told sister it time to go. Or do you need me help you out.

And I would already had the door opened.

Yes, yes, you better not tell anyone. I don't want my business spread all around here.

You already know these girls around here is a player hate. They always jealous of one another. Loved see others head down.

Because some of them in a bad situation so they can feel good. Thinking their better than others. Miss. Joan whispered.

Yeah, I know. Freedom peeking around the corner.

For if a man think himself to be something, when he is nothing, he deceiveth himself.

Did you hear about Mary baby daddy trying take her kids from her? He said she is a bad mother. But I found out he don't want pay her child support to him. So he taking her though hade.

Oh, Ms. Joan. How you found this new out?

Girl, you can't help it when they standing around in the restroom. When her so called best friend telling all her business to others. And laughing about it. I just happened be in there.

While I was doing my business. I couldn't believe what my little ears was hearing. That her buddy would do something like that? It is better to trust in the Lord than to put confidence in man.

Wow, that why I don't fool with these women around here. I know I will catch a case. Because I be ready to whip some behind. So in my case it better just keep my thoughts to myself. Or talking to God about it. I know he won't tell a soul.

Yeah, that true.

Trust in the Lord with all thine heart; and lean not unto thine own understanding.

Well, let me get back to work. So I can go home on time today. Okay! Ms. Joan smile.

Good morning Girls, how was your weekend? Ms. Larry smile.

Girl, I don't think you wanted hear my weekend. It was horrible! Penny getting ready to clock in. Why?

My friend Freedom talk me into go church with her.

Okay, I remembered you was talking about it Friday at lunch. You said going to thinking about it.

Yea, I did. But I wish stay at home.

Ms. Larry, this girl had me going to a funeral. Someone I didn't know.

What?

Na, you joking right.

No, I kidding you not. And the usher had the nerves ask me to sing a solo.

Did you sing it? Miss. Larry smiling, What do you think?

I had a nice red dress on and my black pump. I know I was looking so good. I even put on some make up.

I walk up to the church because I rode the bus there. I started wondering why everyone had on black.

At first it didn't dome on me.

I thought it was 1st Sunday. When they break for his body and drink wine for the blood.

Okay it called communion.

As we was walking up the stairs. I started feeling funny. Something just wasn't right.

Freedom yell here some good seat. We sat in the middle row. All I could think of this girl got me up in here. Looking for a man and I know it wrong. And God going to get us.

The usher yell please clear the aisle.

I look at Freedom shaking my head. I couldn't believe it she got me up in here. This must be a dream please someone wake me up. I don't want me here. I said to myself.

They opened the front doors. And I peek out of it. I saw a black car backing in. And two ushers was standing waiting. And from the rear there was some guys in black suit standing there. When I saw them I knew it was a funeral.

I started looking for a side door. I was about to run up out there. But there was an usher standing at the doors.

I was about choke freedom the death. I ranch over getting ready put my hands round her neck.

The usher yell please stand while the family taking their seat. I had to sit through it. I didn't know who this woman die. Nor their family.

Here I'm sitting there in tears my eyes mad. And ready to break out of there.

I finally got my break that what I thought. What you mean?

Hold on I'm going tell you the rest. But eye on the time.

When they went to viewing the body. I ran into the restroom. I peeking out the door hoping no one standing front of the doors.

I ease out of the restroom thinking I'm going to leave. I didn't care I was leaving Freedom behind.

But an usher tap me on my shoulder. I made it to the door. I had my hand on the door knob getting ready step out. She whispered the family would like everyone view the body.

Maybe you can also sing a solo for the family. I told her okay.

I'll but can I go to the restroom first.

She look over her glasses said okay.

I will wait for you. We can go together you may need some assistance.

I walk slowly back to the restroom. Trying to think away get out this crazy situation. Knowing I don't do funeral. But I had to stay to the end.

Then, Freedom walk up trying joke with me. Do I want to ride in the family car?

Girl, I almost slap her. Because I don't think it was funny. Now, that was a W. O. W weekend you had.

Well, did your friend find the man?

No, I had to go through all that for nothing. But she don't have worry about me anymore. That will never happen again.

Penny you better than me.

Girl, me and her would been fighting up in the church. Tan up the pews

I know we would been in the newspaper. On the front page.

Miss. Larry thank you just made my day. I need a good laugh. Keeping me from going crazy up in here.

Please don't look at me diffidence because I'm not in church. A lot us say we are saint of God.

I bet if you rub them in a wrong way. The old man will rise up. We say that we have no sin, we deceive ourselves, and the truth is not in us.

That why the bible say we suppose to repent daily.

If my people, which are called by my name, shall humble themselves, and pray, and seek my face, and turn from their wicked ways;

Then will I hear from heaven, and will forgive their sin, and will heal their land.

Sometimes we don't know how to control it until too later. Then they have to go back to God get that things right. Or we be in trouble with him.

He knows we isn't perfect because he made us.

For all have sinned, and come short of the glory of God.

Be ye angry, and sin not: let not the sun go down upon your wrath:

If we confess our sins.

He is faithful and just to forgive us our sins, and to cleanse us from all unrighteousness.

And I won't tell a lie I'm isn't there yet. But I'm working on it. I heard a lot of people will say God isn't finished with them.

I wish they stop lying. But if you want be keep. Now God will.

If we say that we fellowship with him, and walk in darkness, we lie and do not the truth.

I want to tell them yes he is. Because he already went to the cross for you and me.

Girl, that just excuse for not getting their self-right with him. Yeah! Miss Larry smile.

Wow, Girl you know that bible.

When Jesus therefore had received the vinegar, he said, It is finished: and he bowed his head, and gave up the ghost.

Yes, I had to know it in my parents house. Penny smile. You just don't know who is on the Lord side.

Yeah, that why you be careful. Because you don't know who watching you. Trying to figure you out.

Yeah, you're right Miss. Larry.

Girl, we better eat our lunch before we be going back to work holding our stomach.

Yeah!

Hey, Ms. Penny what you girls up too?

Nothing, trying to eat a bit or two.

Miss. Berry look over at us. While she was warming up her lunch.

Hey, what you have for lunch? It smell so good.

Oh, that my mother famous chili Miss. Berry smiling.

Okay, you tell your mom put me some up that chili up. They all laugh about it.

Maybe some left if my brother haven't stop by yet.

He need get his self together stop. And stop bring all of his problems to mom. She rise him to take care his self. If he stop putting other before his self. Put God first everything been all right.

Amen Penny look up at her.

But you know some of our children know the way go. Some have to go through the fire and get burn. Before they realize it a fire.

In other word some just don't believe it. Until they have to see or something happen to them.

Yeah, that sound like my oldest sister. She is good example. She is head strong. And seem like she don't care what she do. But God keep sparing her life.

Wow, Miss. Larry

The bell rang.

Girls, that sound like duty calling.

Yea, I just sat down Miss. Berry getting her things together. Lady, I see you tomorrow.

But, if my mother still have some that chili left over. I will bring you a bowl of it in the morning.

Thanks Penny cleaning off the table.

Miss. Berry throw her hand in the air. Heading to the restroom. Penny!

What?

Look at her walk throwing her hips around these guys and smiling. Thinking they going to noticed her. Miss. Larry burst out laughing.

Well, that look so nasty. She need to stop that before that old man of her. Find out he just might put his hand around that neck. Or he break her hip then she won't be able switch anymore.

And chore that devil out of her. Penny, you too funny.

But that woman have that lusting spirit in her.

I think we to need to bring some of my Holy oil tomorrow. And pour all over her pray it out of her.

Miss. Larry look in her purse.

Yeah! Before she be wearing her sunglasses to work. And we already know what happen. So we don't need ask question. Then again that old man of her may not be doing job at home. If you know what I mean.

Oh, we better leave that alone Penny drop head smiling. Well, we better get back to work.

Okay, Miss. Larry thanks again.

Boy, I wish this day was over now. Because it been a long day already.

Penny, penny darling, it time to go home.

What you mean? Miss. Larry

I got to finish this paper.

I been working on it ever since last Thursday. Well, I think it little late try finished now.

What time it is?

Girl, look up on the wall it 3:34pm. Did you hear the bell? No, ma!

Come, on before we end up at the back of the line. You already know sometimes it take us thirty minutes. Before we ranch that old clock. Because people jumping in front of others. Instead they wait their time. They so rude don't care no one but their self.

Okay, okay let me grab my things.

Wow girl, you must been having a good dream.

What you had for lunch?

Aw, aw, I forget Penny trying to get her thought together.

Well, whatever it was you don't need to eat that again. Before they put you out the door.

Why? I do my work.

Yea, but today you slept the day away. I'm glad the boss out of town.

You been in trouble. What was the dream about? If I tell you wouldn't believe me anyway.

Okay, try me! Miss. Larry smile standing over her desk.

I dream, I meet this man had money. I fall in love with him.

But at first I didn't know he own his own business. Because of the way he was dress. But we had so much in comment. We loved the same things.

Wow! That some type of dream. I tell you wouldn't believe me.

Sorry, I don't know about that one. But if you believe it may come true.

Na, it isn't going to happen

I know, I'm not that lucky girl. A man want a simple girl. Penny yell as she walking fast down the hall.

So the last shall be first, and the first last: for many be called but few chosen.

Chapter 8

Don't Judge Me

Bye, Miss. Larry I see you in the morning.

Okay, girl remembered don't eat whatever you had for lunch. When you got home.

Oh, you have joke!

Yea, Miss. Larry smile while she getting into her car. Okay I won't.

All I want to go home now jump in the shower lay across my bed. I hope it will put me to sleep. I don't want be bother.

I finally made it home before I couldn't put my key in the door. My phone ring.

Aw, man I wondered who this? I'm isn't going answered it right now. I'm tried, I'm ready to relax.

I will call them back later.

It better not be Freedom calling me. She know what time I got home. And she know I always like to settle down first before I talk to anyone.

But I better check who calling. It could be an emergency. I look down it was the Donald's law firm.

Wow, I already know what they going to say. I'm not quality fire because I didn't finished school. I'm isn't ready hear some disappointed news. So I will let the voicemail catch the message. And I will listen to it later before I lay down.

Little she know it was Paul confirm her interview on Friday even.

This Paul from the law firm calling on their behalf. If you still interesting in the job please call me back at this number. If you need a ride. I will pick up you.   Thank you.

She finally got a shower and found something to eat.

Lord, should I answer this message or not.

Well, yes let it could be something worth my time.

This Paul I'm calling to confirming your interview on tonight 6pm at Bo's bar q on the 31 and Bullet Ave.

Oh, really I better hurry up call him back. I'm ready get out that old place. And Lord I won't look back.

Hello, is this Paul at the Law firm. Yes this him.

Oh, great I'm glad I caught you. Because I'm returning your call. Yes, I will be there.

Okay, I can't wait meet you there. Because heard they have best bar-q in the city.

Oh, really I haven't been there. Penny smiling

Great, you better get ready lick your fingers. Then again you might bite them off.

Oh yes, we will see about that.

I tell you what just be there. And leave your money at home. Because the company paid for the meal.

Good because this sister don't have it like that anyway. Hey, are you for real? This sound like a dream.

Yes, I prove it. I will send you taxi cab pick you up. Or I pick up you.

Really Mr. Paul.

Please, stop playing with my mind.

Sorry, I don't have time for game. I got replace 3 people because their get ready retired. I hope you will be one them. Thank you. I will see you there.

Penny in shock was speechless.

Okay, if any reasoning you can't make it. Please call me we can reschedule your interview.

Okay, don't worry I will be there Mr. Paul.

Tears running down my face. I can't believe this happen to me.

Let me call freedom tell her the good news. Na, I better wait until get the job first.

Oh, I don't know what to wear. I better start get it together. I don't need to be late.

Boy, I got tell my Miss. Larry this good new in the morning.

Let me get jump in the shower.

Should I call Penny beg for her forgiveness.

I miss her and I don't want her be mad at me. Because we been friends long time.

Girl, I got to find me another job. These people get on my nerves. They always trying put their nose in my business.

And sad part they can't keep their own business together. I can't wait for my man rescue me of this mad hold. As she Freedom stood there at her machine.

Hey, your machine isn't going to turn on by itself.

Girl, you better stop daydreaming again. You already know the boss wife got her eyes on you. You better be careful . Miss. Low yelled.

Okay, I just have a moment. And I'm just ready get up out this place. It getting to the point when I walk in it making me sick. Well, I understand sometimes I feel the same.

But where can I go? I got paid the bills.

Yeah me too. But I know my man going to take care of me. When I catch up with him first.

I'm too old go anywhere else. Miss. Low isn't that old.

I don't know about that one. I was here when they first opened their door. That was back in the 60s.

I was bared 18 year. I should retired long time ago. But I been fooling around with my kids. Now my grand kids think I'm bank. They always trying sell me a sad song. Mother don't have any money to buy me this. Here I'm falling into their little trap.

And I always give in their mom be shaking their head. And telling me don't do it. They need to go find a job. Then they don't need my money or yours.

But I told them I rather give in them. They go out there steal it. They just don't know in due season this bank going out business. And they got to repay their loan back.

Then I will be able taking me a long vacation. And I'm not going tell no one where I going. Maybe I can catch me a young man too.

Freedom burst out laughing. I heard that.

Let me turn this machine on and pray this day be over soon. Amen my sister. Miss. Low throw hand in the air as she walking to her machine. I talk you at lunch.

Okay!

I think I'm going back to church Sunday. Just maybe my man be there. So we can get this dating started. Freedom thought to herself.

Chapter 9

It's Just Happened

Boy, I so excited my friend Rick going out the town. I will have his house alone. First I better drop by the church Sunday. And give God some of my time. And say a little prayer. But while I'm there I can check out the ladies. Maybe I will get noticed.

Peter thinking to his self.

Little he know he will to meet Freedom.

Hey, Peter what you over there grinning about?

Oh, nothing my friend left me his house for a month. And his car. Now you know what going to happen next.

No, what! Mr. Britt.

Girls, girls, I will be on a missioning. Boy that all you think about.

Yeah, until I find a nice one. I'm getting tried being alone.

And the Lord God, said, (It is) not good that the man should be alone; I will make him an help meet for him.

My mother keep asking me when I go to bring some grandbabies home.

I have to keep remembered her first I got find me woman. Who to have kids. Peter stood there.

That sound like my mother use to ask me. No way, what did you tell her or do?

Well, I pray God send me a woman that he wanted me too have. Instead what I want. Mr. Britt smiling

Peter look up with a strange look on his face What?

Mr. Britt! Yeap I did because didn't want any woman.   That isn't right for me.

Boy, you heard me. When you talk to God you better go in detail. Or you just may get someone can be your worthy nightmare.

Because I been there before. Na, not you! Mr. Britt.

Yea, when I was young I thought I found the one. I didn't pray about it. Now if I go back in time think about it was lust. I end up married her trying to do the right things.

Mom told us boys don't play with these girls heart. Because some will get even with you. You don't want it come back to you.

Be not deceived; God is not mocked: for whatsoever a man soweth, that shall he also reap.

And she told my sisters don't play with a man money. They will whip it outback of you. Or kill you.

Now concerning the things whereof ye wrote unto me: it is good for a man not to touch a woman.

Nevertheless, to avoid fornication, let every man have his own wife, and let every woman have her own husband

If you isn't going to married them. So I believe it. Her name sweet Betty until I say I do.

Hey, happen next? Peter smiling I got hear this. I just might learn something here.

She didn't won't clean up the house. Or get a job.

But she use to come on my job on pay day. Had the nerve ask me her my pay check.

Did you give it up? Peter smile

Yeah, I did for a while. Until I found out she wasn't paying the bills. I almost lost the house. I had to get a apart time job make up the money. She mess up. Instead she helping me out getting a job. She rather sit on her lazy behind. On the phone talking whoever.

She always yelling, you the man that isn't her job. Take care of the house. I'm the woman of the house.

One night I just came from work and tired. About to get ready take a shower and relax. She had the nerve pull out the bible showing me some scriptures.

And a man's foes shall be they of his own household.

For even when we were with you, this we commanded you, that if any would not work, neither should he eat.

That what her mother told her. Because her mother didn't work her husband took care of the house.

She thought I suppose to do the same.

Yea, that may be true. But she knew I wasn't making that type of the money like her father maKING.

He was a lawyer.

And here I come alone with 9 to 5 avenger job.

Instead Betty helping me. She just complained every day about something wasn't right. But she wouldn't help me solve the problem. She just made my life a living nightmare.

Boy, I was so glad get rid of her. I dance for joy. I learn my lesson because I didn't pray over nothing.

Now, try me now I praying over everything. No matter what big or little things.

Wow, that something to thinking about. Maybe that my problem I don't have a woman. I never prayer.

Yea, young man. The bell ring.

Aw man, it time go back on this hot floor. Peter walk slowly toward the door.

I know that right. That why I keep praying. I don't have a heat stroke up in here. These people don't care about us. If we hot or cold up in here. Only thing they want us get the work out the door.

I can't wait until my birthday. I got to go my friend. I'll be retiring.

Aw, you going to be miss around here Mr. Britt. Thank for the pep talk.

You always welcome.

I better dress down I don't want her know I'm the owner. Paul thinking to his self. Ask he was getting ready to leave.

Boy, I haven't been on an interview in a long time especially with a woman.

Lord, don't let me mess this thing up. Because I need Someone replace Miss. Cole.

Paul, whispered to his self.

Hey, who was that woman? She have a sweet voice. Is this your new girlfriend?

Na, girl I never met her yet.

I have an interview with her tomorrow.

While a minute. That sound like a date. Gail smile his sectary. You know I can't find a nice girl want be with me. Beside they just wanted my money. When they find out who I'm really is. But it okay, because I know God going to send me that girl soon.

I heard this all my life from my grandmother to my mother. Trust in the Lord and he will give you the desires of your heart. And all mom would talk about Jesus, Jesus.

Commit thy way unto the Lord; trust also in him; he shall bring it to pass.

And mom told me delight thyself also in the Load: and give thee the desires of thine heart.

Yea, that right.

Girl, what you know about that. Paul smile as getting his self together to leave.

My dad keep us in the church. He always saying if I put some Jesus in them. Just maybe, I can keep them out of the street and jail.

Well, it did work? Paul smile.

Yeah, for me but my brother and sister now that another story. They had to try it out. My brother still in jail. And I don't know when he going be release. And my sister have 5 kids now they driving her crazy. Like the she did mom and daddy. When she was younger. She use to slip boys though the window. When she thought mom and daddy was sleep.

One night she almost got me whip by dad. Playing them game lie to him saying it was me slipping in the boys. But dad knew the truth.

A false witness shall not be unpunished, and he that speaketh lies shall not escape.

Wow! Pay back isn't no joke. No! Gail shaking her head.

Well, let me go home now. I see you in the morning. It been long day all I wanted to do lay across my bed. Maybe catch a movie on television.

Okay, don't forgot about tomorrow. What?

You have a date with miss beautiful Penny Lewis.

Oh yea, you right. I better get on out of here. And find some clothes.

Aw, that my darling. Now I know why I hired you. Yes, yes, I know. Because I always keep you on track. Yep! That true.

Thanks! Paul gave her a big hug.

Okay, I think my stomach calling me. It time for dinner.

Girl, you always eating something. You better slow it down. Before I got to help you buy a big bus for you.

Why?

Because you going to be too big riding in your car. Man, get out here talking about me. Gail smiling.

Well, I been look in the mirror I think I'm gain some weight. Plus I noticed some of my clothes is getting to smaller.

Hey, it is good time to fast and pray. So you can drop the weight.

Is not this the fast that I have chosen? To loose the bands of wickedness, to undo the heavy burden, and to let the oppressed go free, and that ye break every yoke?

If someone name Paul going to give me a little rise on my pay check. Then I can buy me some more clothes.

And I don't have too.

Well, I think you better go on this diet. While I think about it. Paul throw his in hand the air.

No, fair Boss.

Bye Gail before I miss my date. Oh, I meant my interview.

Na, you said it right the first time Gail yell. Ask Paul running out of the door. But isn't tonight. It tomorrow after noon. Please don't be late.

Boy, how you forget that so fast?

Chapter 10

Oh What A Night

Hey, Penny I have been trying to call you. I hope you isn't mad at me.

Girl, I forgive you on one condition because we been friends for ever.

Okay, What?

Don't you never ask me come to church with you? Until you check it out first.

Because I don't like funeral especially someone I don't know. Oh, okay I miss hanging out with you.

Well, Freedom did you find that man yet? Or you still dreaming.

Oh, now you have joke.

No, but I'm going back to church Sunday. Maybe I will see him then.

Okay, I just lay here in my bed turn on my television catch the gospel station.

And get my praise on.

Girl, that the lazy way to praise God. Yeah, but it work for me.

For where two or three are gathered together in my name, there am I in the midst of them.

Let me get off this phone. I got catch up on my beautiful rest. And you know already work tomorrow.

Girl, yeah that all I been doing lately.

It time for a girl let down her hair for a while. Maybe catch a good movie and a meal.

I know that right.

Oh, I am sorry I got go.

Where you going? And what you talking about? She didn't answered. But yell I talk to you later.

Bye! Penny throw down the phone. And she ran into the shower. Man, I hope I don't run late. I want this free meal. Plus I'm praying get this job also.

Wow! This how I get forgiving like this? Freedom still holding the phone. And she can't believe Penny did this to me.

Op, now I know she will be mad at me. But she be alright when example what going on. Penny talking to his self. As she put on her make up.

Penny jump on the bus she remember it tomorrow. Yell, please stop the bus.

All the guys whisper at her. One of the guy yell when I take you out.

She yell never. Now have a good night. As she walk off the bus.

Little Penny know Paul going to ask for another date. To confirm that she got the job on Friday night.

Wow, I can't believe this traffic so heavy tonight. I can't to miss this interview. I got to find someone fill in those positions before they leave. Paul thinking trying figure out how he going get through this traffic.

Well, I better not go home until we finished this interview. So I can't be late. Then she problem I'm play game with her.

But Paul still have the interview his mind.

Let me call her back. I know she isn't treating me like that. Yes, I know I mess up her head. But I thought we better than that. Oh Penny with a hold in it.

Freedom getting upset.

Hey, didn't I told her good bye. I got something to do.

And I don't have time to be talking to you right now. Penny hang up the phone.

Wow! I know deserve it. But can a girl get a break here. This don't sound like Penny. I know she up too something.

Why did you rushing me off the phone early? Now you got me about you wondering.

Did you catch a man? And you don't want me to know. No, girl how many time I got to tell you. I'm not looking.

I'm too busy for a man.

Penny! What?

Why you are lying to yourself? Freedom Because I don't believe you. Now that your business.

Just shut up! Before you tell on yourself. Freedom hang up on her.

Why it sound like she getting mad at me? Penny put her phone in her purse. I hoping I don't be late.

Now, she making me wanted snooping around. She know I'm noisy. I want to know what going on with her.

She better not have a man before me.

Wow, why she thinking I got a man. Because she looking don't mean I'm.

Little Penny know Paul going to fall in love with her. But she going to fight it. Because she don't want her heart broken again. And Paul didn't want her know he is owner of the company.

Because he afraid she become a gold digger.

So he going pretend he just avenge guy. He just co- working at the law firm. He just want a beautiful woman who going to love him unconditional.

Maybe someday have a family.

Peter, went back to his machine thinking what Mr. Britt said during lunch.

But I got to shake off this. I'm just tried being alone.

If I pretend I'm rich. I know all type of girls will want to be with me. But I just need the one to be my wife.

Now, that could play in my favor or back fire in my face. And I could end up with no one. When they find out I'm isn't the person that I said I was.

Lord, this a hard one. But I know these girls just don't want avenge Joe. I got have something bring to the table.

Before he knew it the bell rang it was to go home.

Hey, why that look on your face Peter? Man, you got me thinking? Mr. Britt.

Why?

About me playing the ladies. And I don't want end up like you had to go though.

Okay, you going be alright.

Just be yourself and allow God do the rest. Mr. Britt whispered in Peter ear.

Hey, Sis I have an interview tomorrow. Please don't disturb me. If it only an emergency.

Wait a minute why you telling me this? Oh, you finally find a date?

Girl, no! But I wish I could. Paul smile. I guess, these girls thinking I'm bored.

Well, my brother they may be right. Because you always talk about work. Let me give you a secret about a woman.

What?

First of all they love see you smile at them. And tell them beautiful they looks.

Even though they look like hot mess. When you out with them make them your first priority. If another beautiful woman walk by you. Whatever you don't look back at her.

Why? Sis

Because that be rude. A woman want to be first not second. Plus she don't like be in a competition. She thinking she got to fight for your attend. Or be on your phone. If someone call you just simple say let me call you back.

Okay, anything else I need to know. Paul sat there.

Oh, yes don't forget stop by somewhere get them some flowers. Let they know how much you thought of them.

Girl, you should write about how a woman love to be broom. And be treated like a queen. I bet it will sell it out in the same day.

Because some men just don't know. Some of these men didn't have a father in their life.

Nor had someone taught them how treat to a lady. I saw too many our uncles abused their women.

I thanks for mom didn't allow it happen to her. Wow, sis so why you don't have a man yourself. Oh, I just told you why?

Too many these boys still don't want grow up.

Become a man who know their place. And how to be a father to his own children. Instead take care other men children.

I'm tried being that woman. I rather be alone then allow another man come into my life. Play with my mind again making promises. They won't keep it. Plus you know I have Red here watching me.

And I know, I mess up in my past as younger.

When I was a child, I spoke as a child, I thought as a child: but when I became a man,

I put away childish things.'

But I want to thank God step in giving another chance make things right.

I want her be the woman God use for his glory.

Plus I want her know she have the right. She don't have to accept anything from a man just be with him.

Okay, girl you start sound like mom now. The both burst out laugh.

I just want to best for my children. Sis smile I know that why I haven't had any kids yet.

Because I see these crazy baby mom. They always love the drama. And I can't deal with it.

Some of them will put their hands on you. Try make you do something bad to them. That what happen to our cousin Louis. He got tired of it. He almost went to jail. And the girl started accusing him that he was cheating on her.

But that wasn't true he had to work a lot over time on the job.

When things hit the fan she was the one cheating on him. Until this day the family wondering if the children is his. Now she put him on child support.

Now he had to go get another job just to pay it.

And she refused allow him spend time with them alone. Because she afraid he would go get a blood test on them. And find out the truth.

Now you see why. Sis

Yea, that mess up. A woman shouldn't do a man like that. Now if that man isn't trying do right by his children. That another story then you got the right take act to protect the children.

But if any provide not for his own, and specially for those of his own house, he hath denied the faith, and is worse than an infidel.

You right.

Well, sis I got go and fined me some clothes for tonight. Okay, why you can throw anything on. And you be fine.

Aw, that not me brother. I got get my hair done, nails and especially my feet done too. That be the first thing a man look at. If you wearing high heel with the toes sticking out. I got look my best.

That why some women can't get a date because they stop caring about their selves. When they start having kids. Maybe was in a bad relationship. Or they going into dispersion. Thinking no one want them anymore. But I realize you don't know who watching you. Maybe they looking for mate. I know I need a strong a man help me raise my two kids.

Yea, amen to that. My Sis because getting they out hand. A good man need step in help you put them back in a child place.

My son, hear the instruction of thy father, and forsake not the law of the mother.

Oh, I don't want no one know I'm the owner.

Maybe I can catch a date after I finished my interview. I know a lot women going to be there. Maybe I can take few number down. You never know who looking for Godly man.

Oh, you looking now?

Yea, sis just tired been alone. In this big house I thought about it. Just buy me a smaller house. Because it just me right now. I don't really need it.

Brother, how could you sell it when mom gave it to you?

The righteous shall inherit the land, and dwell therein forever.

Did you forget what she said? if don't want live in the house. Let a family member live in it.

Yeah, you're right.

Hey sis, let me get off this phone get myself together. Or I might go by the church it bible study tonight.

Okay, bye. If you do? Say a pray for me. Okay but it good you come alone sometimes. And you never know who maybe looking. Plus it be good the kids' sake. Paul hang up his phone.

Well, I'm bored let me put on some clothes. Maybe I go to bible study tonight. So can be ready if my man ask me question about the bible. I won't look foolish. Freedom thinking to herself.

Little Freedom know she will going run into Paul.

Hey, Penny how was your day?

Oh, it wasn't too bad. It just I'm getting tired of this old job. Wish I had sometimes little better paying more and some better benefit.

Girl, I know right. When I get this man together. I won't worry about it anymore.

Because I won't have to work so hard. If I just keep him happy. I know you crazy. What about cooking and clean up the house. Freedom.

Girl, that not me! He better already have a maiden. I don't do house work. It may mess up my nails.

I think I need to put Mrs. Donnie on speed dial. Why?

We may have put you in that place they call it crazy house. Na, I'm fine.

Yeah, I know I been to your house. You have clothes everywhere.

Hey, you caught me getting ready do my laundry. Yea, right who you trying to fooling yourself.

Freedom!

What?

Clean up that dirty house. No man want come over your house got sit on clothes. And maybe you be surprise what you find under them.

Bye girl, I got to get ready for bible study. Maybe my man be there. And that my opportunity talk to him get this date started.

Okay, don't think about it? What?

Asking me do I want to go with you? Let spell it capitol N and small o I think that mean No.

I don't need another nightmare. I didn't sleep for 3 days. Now I'm good.

I'll talk with later. Freedom.

Mr. Britt, I see you in the morning. Maybe I go to church today is Wednesday right?

Yeah!

It bible study.

Oh, Peter are you okay?

Yes sir! Maybe some women be there. Or my dream girl waiting on me.

Man, you are crazy. Trying catch a woman at church.

Yea, I know you heard that old saying.

No, you tell me.

Mr. Britt, come on I know you heard it too. They say all the good girls go to church.

And I'm going find out is that old saying is true. Peter

Sir!

Can I pray with you? Yes, I love that. Mr. Britt.

Okay, Lord this is my friend Peter. Look out for him these women out there won't whip his behind. For Playing game with their heart. I don't want see him coming to work with black eyes. Lord, Lord nor a big lip because one of these women hit him. In Jesus name Amen

Hey, don't be fool every woman go to church. Don't mean everyone is good.

I know some of the women belong to my church. They shout on Sunday. But if you step on their toes on Monday. They will cut you up. I know this guy name Gerry use to come to the church.

He was dating one of the Lady there. She found out this young girl trying to talk him.

It was so bad.

Well, what happen? Peter stood there with a serious look on his face.

One Sunday the young girl walk in the church.

The church was full. It was hard to find a place to sit.

I guess the woman saw her came in she got up with her big black bible in her hand. Walk up to the girl hit upside her head. The girl fall out she didn't see it coming.

Everyone was in shock. Even the Pastor didn't know what to say. It was middle of the service.

Man, if you knew this woman she come in the church singing the Lord is good. And dancing all around it.

Wow! Mr. Britt are you for real. Yeah!

Someone took pictures of the lady and the girl while she was getting up off the floor.

The old ladies yell get this devil out of here.

I wondering what the guy felt when he heard about it.

Oh, he knew something going to happen soon or later. That probably why he didn't show up that Sunday.

Well, Mr. Britt I don't blame him. Or they would've whip his behind for playing game with them.

He must heard that old song.

What song?

Run for your life and don't look back. The both burst out laughing.

Hey, Peter don't let this be you.

Na, I can't handle more than one woman at a time.

Let no man deceive you with vain words: for because of these things cometh the wrath of God upon the children of disobedience.

Yea, why not I got more time on my hand then money. I'll let you know happen in the morning.

First, I better go buy me another bible. It wouldn't look right if I walk in without it.

Well, yea that true.

Bye, I bet you keep your mother on her knees. Because you so lost I hope while you there you will get yourself together

Mr. Britt thank you.

Yea, me too.

I better go ahead find something to wear. For my interview tonight. Maybe I wear a dress. Na, he maybe think I'm easy. Well, I got it. I will wear my blue jean outfit. Just maybe I'm be okay.

The phone rang.

Hello, Freedom I thought I said good bye for tonight.

Oh, yes you did but I got to know. What?

Why we can't hang out tomorrow? Saturday I may need my rest for Sunday. Because if my man don't show up for church tonight. I got to run him down to get his number. I'm getting tired waiting on him. I got step up my game before I lose him.

Freedom try figure this thing.

Girl, what I'm going to do with you?

Penny, Just love me because I'm who I am. I know you lost your mind. Freedom

Girl, go to sleep because I'm not going to tell. Okay, but I got ready to meet my man at church. I know he better be there. He know I miss him.

Bye this time I'm going to turn off my phone.

Just maybe I will tell you about it Saturday while we hanging out.

Yea, yea Freedom hang up the phone. I better hurry get dress. And get to the bus stop.

So I won't be late for church. I want to get there early so can get good seat.

Just maybe he already there. And I can sit by him and slip him my number.

By that time the phone rang. I knew Penny going to change her mind. She wanted come to church with me. So I better answer it.

Hey Girl, did you change your mind? What you talking about? This your mother. Oh, sorry mom.

I thought you was Penny.

Hey, did you forgot something? No, mom.

Oh yes, you did? What?

You promise to stop by and help me clean up your old room. Oh, my god. I can't tonight. I'm on my way to church.

What? Freedom! Did you trip on something? And bump your head.

Na, mom I just going to bible study. Is something wrong with that?

Yea, Girl, because you never like going. I and your daddy had to drag you in almost every Sunday. Unlet the church having a dinner. And your brother too.

I know you up to something. You can't fool me.

Did Penny call you?

No, why? I don't know her like that.

Oh, what she got something to tell me?

No, no but sorry I got to go before I be late. Okay, see how my own daughter do me?

What mom? Please don't do this me make me feel guilt. Oh, no but she don't have time for me.

It okay, when someone name Freedom drop by the house. Asking for something to eat.

I'm going to say politely as your daddy. And you already know what he going to say.

You better go on a fast it won't hurt you lose little weight. For more if you start bring in something. You can carry something out.

Yes, mom, I got go now. I don't want miss this bus. Okay, bye girl you should've learn how to drive a car.

Instead catching that old bus. What?

That is another bills and I don't need that right now. Mom, why you don't know how drive yourself?

Girl, just shut up. I been waiting on your father teach me for years. And he always come up with an excuses.

He thought he was smart then me. And I let him thinking it. Why?

Because I couldn't catch him running behind these old crazy women.

All my friends came back tell me they saw him all over the town.

He had a different women in his car.

Well, maybe that was a good thing on his behalf. I didn't know how to driver. Because I probably be in jail and he be in hade. He be wishing for a piece of ice cool his self-down.

Aw, mom you know daddy love you.

Yea, right he just love what I can do for him.

Girl, you better be careful out there. Why mom?

You just might be dating your brother.

Mom, stop playing dad isn't like that. My dad are faithful to you. You know dad is a God fearing man.

Be not wise in thine own eyes: fear the Lord, and apart from evil. Mom burst out laughing.

Yea, right every time it start raining heavy and lighting.

Why your father grab his bible and start praying. Sometimes he be speaking in tongues. Yelling please

Lord, stop the thunder and lighting. I can't take it anymore. I'll be good. Soon it over he doing the same thing again.

Hold up and wait minute before you jump on that bus. How you know your father say he was working late.

But he don't know I use to peek at his pay check. And the hour and the money doesn't add up.

Oh, okay I'm sorry.

Yeah, sometimes the devil rise up in me. I just want to slap the holy ghost out of him. For all the lying he told me. I don't think he got it anyway. If so I don't show it toward me. But he want everyone else think he does.

Oh, mom you know that be wrong. And God won't like it. Well, that may be true. But it make feel good.

Bye, mom I'm going to pray for you.

Oh, thanks but please don't leave your old daddy out. Okay Mom I will.

I finally got to church I jump off the bus. Hoping I'm isn't late because I got catch this man tonight. Freedom thinking as she walking up the stairs fast.

Now, I better stop play around throw some clothes on before I'm be late. And I might miss my opportunity. Because I know it going be some ladies there. Peter thinking while getting in the shower.

I hope this traffic don't be heavy tonight. I got ready for bible study. I don't want miss a word. It just maybe for me. I need a words. If I meet a lady in church. I got find something to talk about. What is a good thing then talk about the bible?

Who is wise man and endued with knowledge among you? Let him shew out of a good conversation his work with meekness of wisdom. Paul jump into the car.

Well, finally that girl letting me rest. I don't want be too tired when I have my interview tomorrow. Penny grab her a night snack.

Good morning, Penny!

Girl, where going looking like at? Morning, Miss.Larry.

Oh, I just thought I put on some clothes today. Okay, I thought you going to another funeral.

Who die? Penny turn around look up side her head.

Na, isn't going to happen until it my own. I hope I won't know it.

Girl, don't play. My friend (Freedom) already mess up my head. I still have nightmares because of that.

No, thanks!

Oh, I got some business I got to take care after work. And I didn't want to go back home change. I'm afraid I'll be late.

Wow, you mean you have a date.

No, no Freedom ask me the same question. Last night because I told we can't hang out with her.

Girl, who you trying fool? Dressing like that. No one so how do I look?

You look great. But you better learn how to walk in those hi. I hate see you on your back looking up at ceiling.

Yea, I know it been a long time since I wore these shoes. Hey, you better stop in by the office before walk on the floor. Why? Miss. Larry.

Oh to check on your insurance to see if it still good. You just might needed.

Now, you have joke.

Yea, I need a good laugh this morning. Why?

Because it was so hard come up in here. I sat at the end of my bed. Asking myself why me?

Lord, I have to come up in the place. Day after day have to put up with the drama.

A soft voice whispered in my ears. You isn't coming for yourself anymore. But my people need you. They is lack of knowledge.

And they need someone show them the way.

If any of you lack wisdom, let him ask of God, that giveth to all men liberally, and upbraideth not; and it shall be given him.

I chose you to handle my business for me. Because I know they love your present. Yes, I know you feel like you wasting your time when you tell them about me.

Oh, you just don't know a lot appreciate the word. Because of you many started back praising me.

Even some of younger looking up to you. Ready to hear the word for the day. Said the Lord.

That what made me come today. Miss.Larry

Well, I'm glad you did because I need a word for today. Girl, just be yourself and don't change for no one.

Hey, what you mean? I'm being myself.

Miss.Larry throw her hand in the air. And walk out the break room.

But, but why you say that? I'm confuse Miss. Larry.

The bell rang.

I better go work before I be late again.

Hey, girl where you going? Are you going back to another funeral? And I hope you know the person this time.

You stop playing with me too. Mrs. Larry already ask me the same thing.

Do I look like I'm going to a funeral? Maybe I need run back home change. Penny stood there.

Well, I'm surprise to see you in a dress.

No, if you must I got know why dress like this?

Come, closer I got some business take care. Before I go home today.

Okay, you must got a date.

And you don't want your friend like me to know. Danny go to work. I just may tell you later.

Right, I better finished up some back projects. Before I living be in a shelter.

I will talk with you later.

Boy, why everyone thinking I'm going on a date.

I don't have a man on my mind. But I do have my mind on making more money.

I'm sick of tried working under pay and especially under appreciate. Penny whispered to herself. As she going to her desk.

I wish this day over. So I stick my lip into some bar –q.

I pray Lord this interview go well. I can use the extra cash. Maybe I can take a real vacation for a change. Instead sitting around the house looking brochure wishing I was there. Laying on the beach looking at the guys passing by. They waving at me. Delight thyself also in the Lord: and he shall give thee the desires of thine heart.

Hey, Penny are you going home today? What? Danny!

Girl, you need to stop daydreaming. And let go home. The bell rang.

Oh, I better get up before I run late.

What going on with you isn't yourself today? Danny stood over her desk.

I have so much running through my mind. Right now I can't think straight.

I promise, Monday be alright.

Sorry, I get go to catch this bus. Okay, Penny!

Before I could make it to the clock my phone rang.

Aw, man this better not be Freedom trying to call me. I better see who calling me.

It was the Law firm.

Oh, I hope they isn't going cancel the interview. Hello,

Is this Penny Louis. Yes, this she.

I wanted you know I have a car waiting for you down stairs. What are you for real? But how youknow where I'm working at. Oh, it your application.

Oh, I'm so silly! Okay thanks.

But I will catch the bus. Because this sister really don't have the fare.

No, please it no cost to you. The company will take of it.

Okay, please don't send me a bill me later. Miss. You too funny.

I'm on my way down soon I clock out.

Hey, did you see Penny getting in the beautiful car?

Oh yes, I'm wondering what she getting herself into? Miss.Larry whispered over to Danny.

Why you got to know her business? As Danny walking out. Yea! Look that my friend I'm trying to look out for safe.

Oh, okay sorry. Miss. Larry let me go home.

I hope something good come out of it. She deserve it. I'll see her Monday morning.

Chapter 11

The Blessing

Wow, I can't believe my eyes. Someone go out their way for me. Hello, Sir.

Now Lord, I need this job.

Sorry, I'm keep asking. I just want a change in my life.

I promise, I will work on going back to church. But, but I won't go with Freedom again. She mess up my head.

It feel so good that I don't have to ride that old bus. People talking loud, and some don't know what soap and water for. This must be a dream. Let me shake myself make sure I'm isn't sleep. I'm in this beautiful car. I can stretch out in it.

Oh, it have a television in it too. Now that going to make me wanted stay in the car. I can watch my favorite show. I never have to go home. Just ride until get tired of it.

Ma, we are here.

Aw man, I just getting comfort kicking back. I'm enjoying the ride.

Okay, but you must promise me. We can do this again. Penny, getting out the car.

Yes, ma I promise.

Girl, go have you some fun. I know their bar-q is great. You better prepare yourself you may not be able walk out. It going to make you lick you fingers.

I try it and I ate some so much. It put me asleep at the table. The waitress had to wake me.

Okay, I'll thanks for the ride.

I know Freedom won't know how to act. If she can see me now. I think I will take a few pictures. It just mess up her head.

Miss, someone waiting for you inside. Okay!

I walk in this place was so big. And the food was smelling good. I heard someone call my name.

Miss. Penny!

Yes, I look around there a tall handsome man smiling. My name Paul.

Okay, this the man behind the phone.

Yeah! And you the beautiful lady. I'm been waiting to meet. I'm the one only Miss. Penny. She smile.

I hope my makeup don't run down my face. Because I'm so nerve. She whispered.

Oh, oh, sorry please let pull your chair out for you.

Okay, you are a real gentleman?

Well, yea ma, my mother didn't play that. She taught her boys how treat a woman.

Alright mom. I give her nine point for that.

I would like to meet her someday. Let know her she did a fine job here.

Sorry, she die two years ago.

Oh, sorry I'm running my mouth to much. Please forgive me.

No, no, I'm enjoyed your company.

It been a long time since I interview someone.

First of all let order dinner. Then I will start the interview. Okay, Penny grab a menu off the table. Started looking at it.

Wow, it very expensive are you sure you wanted eat here. One of these meal it take my hold pay check to pay it.

Yes!

Paul, burst of out laugh.

What so funny? She look at him. Oh, I'm sorry forgive me.

It okay, but I'm for real. I been at this job over ten years. Working myself to death. And they don't want give you a rise. When they do give you a rise the taxes and your insurance go up. My pay check look the same just maybe a few dollar more.

Wow, I understand.

A lot companies do that hoping you get mad enough so you will quit.

So they can hire someone in your place pay them less money and benefit.

I don't think that isn't fair. God going to take care them. For cheating their employees.

Be not deceived; God is not mocked: for whatsoever a man soweth, that shall he also reap.

For he that soweth to his flesh reap corruption; but he that soweth to the Spirit shall of the Spirit reap life everylasting.

And some don't care if you have a family you must provide for. But you better believe their family don't have to want for nothing. I know what it mean when you have to do without. My mother taught us you can't have everything you see. And I had a lot friends I grow up with theirs parent struggle trying keep bread on their table. And roof over their head. But God always step in at the right time. They never miss a meal. Because they was a praying family.

I know sometime I be over my friend house.

His mother polite told me if you want to play with John. You must come in pray with him a few minute.

I was shock.

I had to get on my knee to pray just to play.

My opinion on that if you have faithful people take care you. You should do them right. Because they really help you carrying the load.

But my God shall supply all your need according to riches in glory by Christ Jesus.

Yes, you can replace people. But the question is do they have your best interesting? Or they just out to take your money.

For the love of money is the root of all evil: which while some coveted after, they have erred from the faith, and pierced themselves through with many sorrows. Well, yes that true.

But wait a minute I thought you supposedly be interview me. Oh, I sorry couldn't help myself.

Because I'm a big fan of the Lord. Sometimes I can't stop talking about him.

Well, can you work a computer? Yes!

Take messages on the phone. Yes!

Can you work long hours to finished a project. Yes! I could use some of the over time.

Why you think you be the right person for this job? I'm dedication to my work.

Okay!

Penny, can you with others without start a problem?

Is that trick qustion? Penny smile.

Well, you want the true or a lie? Please the truth!

Yes, I can. But some people difficult to work with. I know that right! Paul sat back

If a problem come up. How would you handle it?

First of all pull them aside and try reasoning with them. If that doesn't work. I will talk to the supervisor to handle it. Before it become bigger problem.

Okay, great answered.

Do you have transportation?

No, but if I get this job. I'm going to buy a car. And learned how drive it. I'm getting tired of ride that old bus. Sometimes the bus run late.

And I can't afford it right now because I'm single. I must pay my own bills.

Oh, you single. Paul smile.

Yes, I am. And I don't have time babysitting. What?

Most of the men I dated in the past. All they wanted me take care of them. They didn't want together work. And I already have enough on my plate.

I don't need any death weight trying to pull me down. Well, I do understand.

Hey, how we get on this subject about my life.

Okay, now on it what about you? Penny look up at him. Oh, I'm very single, no children yet.

All the women I dated they told me I all talk about the job.

And I was bored.

Well, I don't think that. But I know you love the Lord.

I kind of like that in a man. If I was looking for a man Penny face light up.

Because I grow up going to church. But I got tired of hearing the message every Sunday. If don't repent you going to hell. It got too much for me. So I just stop going. But I still worship God in my bed room every Sunday. And read my bible daily.

Okay, Paul start smiling. And he forget was interview. Hey, who name you Penny?

Oh, my mother said I came out like shining golden brown penny.

And my father give me my first birthday a necklace with a penny with a hold in it. I still wear it today.

Wow, it different. But a pretty name. Well, who name you Paul?

My mother too I guess she love going to church. She got my name from the bible. Praying I would become a great leader. Like the Apostle Paul was a great leader.

By this time Paul phone rang.

Aw man, who calling me now. I really don't want be bought. Yes I understand!

Go ahead answered it could an emergency.

Okay, I will excuse me.

It my sister I told her please don't call tonight. I'll be out. I got to call her.

Hey, what going on? Sis.

I'm sorry for calling you. But little Tony fall in the bathtub. While was playing in the bathroom. Instead he use it. He need to go the emergency room. To make sure he didn't break any bone.

Okay, I'm go my way. Okay, thanks. Bro.

Sorry, I break up your date.

There go Sis. I talk you a few minute.

Oh, man I'm just beginning having some fun. Now this happen to me. Paul had a frown on his face.

Aw, what wrong?

My nephew fall in the bathtub. While her was playing in the bathroom. Instead he use it. And I must take him to the emergency room. I pray he didn't break any bone.

Well, I know I'm be spend my rest of night.

Oh, sorry do you want some company? Penny ask. Let me call you a cab. So you have a ride home.

Oh, don't worry about me.

Na, I'll be okay.

Just go take care your nephew. But thank anyway.

Okay!

Because you going need your rest. I need you stop by the office. Monday morning finished up your application. And get ready take your drug test.

What! Penny jump up and kiss him on his cheap. Wow, what that for?

Yes, I think you be great for the job. Paul smile as he getting walking out the door.

Penny had tears in her eyes.

Hey why you crying?

Because God answered my prayer.

If ye abide in me and my words abide in you, ye shall ask what ye will, and it shall be done unto you.

Miss. Penny I will see you Monday.

Wow, what kind of woman put other before herself?

I want to get to know her better. Maybe she will be the one. And I like the way she talk, how she take time out listening to me.

She have a beautiful smile.

Boy, that man look so fine. And something about this man. He isn't like the other guys. I went out with.

I think I want a date with this man. I want to know more about him.

Let me shut up this man don't want a woman like me. I'm not rich nor beautiful.

I better call Freedom tell her what happen to me. Aw, man my phone is dead.

Well, I will call her in the morning.

O wow, how can I break this news to Miss. Larry and Danny? I'm leaving the company.

I finally made it to the church. I hope this man be here. Let me find a seat before all the good seat be gone.

Freedom start pretending she are reading her bible. But at the same time looking up. Hoping this man show up.

Boy, I better hurry up get there before the service start. Maybe I can get some numbers. Peter jump in his friend car.

Why this night someone had to have a wreck? Got this traffic held up. But I hope no one got hurt. Now I'm going to be late. Peter finally made it.

Excuse me may I sit here.

Freedom said yes before she realize who was sitting by her. When she look up her mouth drop. It was the man she been running behind him.

What can I say to him let him know I want his number.

She started thinking all type of ways to get his attend. And she forget where she was.

Please stand for the prayer and the reading of the words.

If you have your bible study book. Please turn to page 15. And please share with other. But those who don't have one.

Our subject will be talk about how others can deceive you. If don't be careful.

I will read couple scriptures.

Freedom and Peter grab their bible at the same time. The both was face to face smiling at one another.

Psalms 52: 2 Thy tongue deviseth mischiefs; like a sharp razor, working deceitfully.

Proverbs 12:22 Lying lips are abomination to the Lord: but they that deal truly are his delight.

Okay, we made eyes contract. I think I can slip my number to him. Freedom whispered to herself.

Oh, I know I can get this number. But I got find the right timing. Or he may run the other way.

Then again she might be married or have a boyfriend.

So I better be careful what I say to her. First let me look to see if she are wearing a ring. Peter thinking to his self.

Wow, this man smell so good. I wish Penny can see me now sitting by my man.

Oh, I need get a picture of us sitting together. So Penny can believe me. Let me ease my phone out of my purse. Maybe I can steal a picture when he turn his back around. Hoping he don't catch me. It could be embarrassed.

I hope bible study don't last too long. And I hope she don't run out of here before I can ask for her number.

Boy, I been waiting so long to see this man.

Please Lord, don't let him be already marriage or have someone.

Because I know he have big bank(money). I'm trying get some it. God you already know my story. This sister tried of working. I want someone take care of me.

Looking at his watch, rings and that necklace he is wearing. It doesn't look cheap.

But little she know Peter wearing his friend's Doug jewelry. Who really have got the bank? (money)

So I pretend looking in my bible. I acting like I was looking for a piece of paper. Knowing I didn't have none.

Excuse could I borrow a sheet of paper. So I can take some note.

Oh, yes I look up at him smile.

Here you go. Sorry it my number on it.

I hope you don't mine.

No, thanks but I need a pen too. Peter whispered. Oh okay!

Wow, this our first conversation. I can't wait tell Penny about it. Well, now I don't have to ask her for her number.

Oh, wait a minute she may be trying to set me up.

But I just play alone with her little game. Then again it could be something good come of it.

Well, I don't have to slip my number in her purse. Peter whispered to his self.

Excuse me are you talking to me? Oh, sorry no.

Okay Freedom lean over whispered.

Finally the bible study over.

Freedom gathered her things and putting away her bible. Please may I help you put on your coat?

Sure!

I can't believe this man start taking some interest in me. Oh, by the way what your name?

Freedom and you.

Peter! It nice to meet you.

Thanks same to you. Freedom smile.

Wow, are you like the man in the bible name Peter? He burst out laughing.

What?

Now that funny?

Well, I thought it will put a smile on your face. Oh, you did. I don't smile a lot.

Why?

I don't know.

Maybe I don't have anything smile about. Peter just stood here. Oh, yes! You do I know God been good to you?

Well, yes! I can't complained about that. Peter smile.

Oh, I smile at everything let other know I'm a lovely person. Oh, that so. Peter look down at her.

Yeah!

I want to find out.

You say what? Freedom eyes got big.

Yes, I'm asking you maybe we can try get to know each other. Are you for real? Or you just playing with my head.

No, here my number call me.

Maybe we can go to dinner. Peter smile as he walk out the door. Okay, Freedom said in a soft voice.

Lord, you just answered my prayer. I must doing something right.

She had tears in her eyes.

I'm going to be rich. And I have someone to care of me. I see myself shopping, living in a big house, and having a maiden cooking, cleaning my house.

Little know she is going get her feeling hurt.

Thinking this man got money by the way he look and dress. But he just like her hoping find someone have money too.

But be ye doers of the word, and not hearers only, deceiving your own selves.

Wow, I got to tell Mr. Britt about this.

I hope she have some money too. She look like she worth a million dollar. Maybe she dress down so others won't know who she is.

Because this brother tried working so hard. Just maybe I can be like my friend Doug. Don't have to worry about anything.

Now I'm going to sit back wait on her call me.

Okay! Don't fool yourself. Mr. Britt smile as he grab him a cup of coffee.

What you mean?

She might be trying fool you. To see what you can do for her. Well, in that case I well watch I say to her.

Thanks, for the advice. Your welcome.

I better hurry up drinking this coffee. And run to the bathroom before I start up my day. I'm get old can't be trying my machine. And I got run to the bathroom at same time. Mr. Britt walking fast.

Chapter 12

Wow, I must Be dreaming

Wow, what a night my dream come true. I got call Penny to tell her. I got my man name and his number. And I can't wait for our first date. I got to buy something special. Show him I can dress for the occasion. Freedom thought to herself. As walking out the door.

Now I'm going to show Penny who the woman?

Penny finally got home. Boy thank you Lord for a wondering for night with a fine man. Especially you answered my prayer. Now Lord I'm going make my way back to church.

Hey, sis let go got him to the emergency room. Okay, I ready! Aw, brother I'm so sorry this happen. Sis!

What?

It okay. You know family come first. But I was enjoyed myself.

For the first in a long time. And she isn't like those others women I try to date in the past.

What you Bro? As they wait see a doctor.

Because she didn't try take advance of me. I told her get whatever wanted to eat. She started complaining about the price. And she order the cheaper thing on the menu. Plus she ask for a glass of water. But I odered her club soda instead.

Now that mess my head up. Because the other women try get the higher thing on the menu. And they pick over the food. And they throw half of it away. I was kind of upset about that. At least they could've took it home with them.

Oh, yep! Bro she could've playing with you act like she isn't about the money. Until she know she got you wrap around her thumb. Then start asking for things.

Na, sis I think you wrong about her. Plus she is my new hire.

What? Let see how this going to turn out. When she find out you owner of the company.

Oh, I got that cover to. Because I'm going to which place with Rick. I'm going to let him become me for a while. Plus this be a good time trains for him. If something would happen to me. I need someone I can trust him handle my business. After that I'm going to surprise him for his birthday. I'm going to give him a peace of the stock. Because he been with me ever since I open the law firm. And I think I owe him that.

Therefore said he unto them, The harvest truly is great, but the labourers are few: pray ye therefore the Lord of the harvest, that he would send forth labourers into his harvest.

Plus, he been a true friends. And I thank God for him. Yes, we fight sometimes but he keep my focus. Also he save the bussiness many time.

Iron sharpeneth iron; so a man sharpeneth the countenance of his friend.

Okay!

Boy, I can't got woman out of my mind. But I can't let her know how I'm beginning feel about her. Paul smiling to his self.

Oh, I better keep an eye on my brother. I hope isn't a gold digger out for his money. Plus he just met her too. Sis. Whispered to herself.

So Monday I will back off. And I will allow Gail train her.

As I open the door I saw my man getting in his beautiful blue car.

I bet this cost him a pretty penny.

Boy, I can't wait soon I'll be riding with him. No more bus.

I won't have to wait on in the hot heat nor the cold weather. And I won't be around weird peoples be out here too. And I don't what they might try do to me.

That why I thank God for his protect

God is our refuge and strength, a very present help in trouble. Oh, wait a minute I better not call her this time of night. She will be mad I'm break up her sleep.

I just wait call her in the morning.

I better hurry up got in the shower when I get home. As Freedom waiting on the bus.

The next morning Penny jump out of her bed. And ran in the shower put some clothes on.

The phone ring.

I bet this Freedom trying call me. Girl, I have some news to tell you. Me too! Penny yarning.

You go first they both said it at the same time. Hello, hello Freedom, What going with your phone?

Hey, Penny, Penny what wrong with your phone? Let see if my phone charge up.

Aw, man my phone is dead. I forgot to put on charger last night. I better put it on the charger before I hit this door trying go to work. And I hope it be ready by my first break at work.

Wow, this jack up I forget to put my phone on the charger. I really want her know what happen to me.

Oh, well I guess I call Freedom back on my lunch break. My phone should be charge.

Now Lord, how I'll going to tell my friends that I'm leaving. Penny thinking while getting ready lock her door. I'm going to miss them. But I got to look out for myself.

If you abide in Me, and my words abide in you, ask whatever you wish, and it will be done for you.

Good morning, Miss Larry How was your weekend?

Girl, it started off bad and at the end it got better. Hey, what you mean?

My oldest son get into auto accident. We all rush to the hospital.

They saying be prepared yourself for the worth. He may not make it through the night.

Girl, my heart drop I couldn't breathe. I thought I was going to be admired too in the hospital But when I caught my breath.

Only thing cross my mind jump into my closet started praying. But thou, when thou prayest, enter into thy closet, and when thou hast shut the door, pray to thy Father which is in secret; and thy Father which seeth in secret shall reward thee openly. Then shall ye call upon me, and ye shall go and pray unto me, and I will hearken unto you.

My son and daughter run into the house looking for me. And they yelling my name. All could say Jesus please go before me heal my son.

So I ran out my room jump into the car. When I got there to the hospital.

I ask for my son.

The nurse look at me strange. What your son name Carl L. Jones.

The young man came in had a car accident. Yes, ma!

Wow! She have a funny look on her face.

Girl, I just close my eyes. Praying that he okay. Ma, come go with me.

I got to say there must be a God looking out for him. Yes, I know all that. I'm a praying mother.

Please tell me what you saying.

Okay, ma your son didn't have any scratches on him.

All I could do fall on my knees just thanking God for sparing my boy life.

When I saw him. He promise me he going back to church. And turn his life around.

Hey mom, I know that God just warning me.

Pride goeth before destruction, and an haughty spirit before a fall.

I'm isn't going take any more chances. The Lord may allow the emery take me out the next time.

I want to be ready.

Mom, remembered what Grandma said before she passed away.

I know you thought I wasn't listening. But I was I just wasn't ready to make that change.

Grandma, use to yell at me when I got into trouble. Boy, you know God saw you. And he don't like it.

You better get it together before he come back. I told her I had time because I'm still young.

Then she said but that may be true. But she let ask me one question.

I look up at her.

Did you read anywhere or someone told you when Jesus coming back?

I drop my head said no ma.

For yourselves know perfectly that the day of the Lord so cometh as a thief in the night.

Then she grab the belt started whipping my behind. She yell I'm doing this because I love you.

He that spareth his rod hateth his son: but he that loveth him chasteneth him betimes.

Girl, I wanted shout all over the hospital. When I heard the new my truning his life around. But they problem think I'm lost my mind. And put me in a strait jacket.

And pull down my pant hit me twice with a needle to clam me down.

Penny burst out laughing. I know needle would've hurted. Wow, now that sound like our God.

So how was your weekend? Oh, it was great.

The bell rang.

Hey, I got clock in before I be late.

I will tell about it during break time. Okay, Miss. Larry went in the restroom.

By that time I step on the floor. Every one looking at me. Okay, What I do this time. I whispered.

As I walked toward my desk. It was my picture on my desk.

Now my heart was really pumping fast. I know I'm in trouble about something. Well I better prepare myself for this bad news.

The letter said you are the employee of the month. You will received a 100 dollar bonus on your next pay check.

They all started clapping their hands and yelling good job.

I drop my head in tears. Now this going to make it harder to leave.

Why you crying? Danny walk up gave me a hug.

Congratulation, you deserve it. Because you are a harder worker. You don't mind stay over get the job done.

Wow, I didn't see it come. Now, Lord why?

I had to turn my head. I broke down in tear because God answered my prayer.

Therefore I say unto you, What things soever ye desire, when ye pray, believe that ye receive them, and ye shall have them.

By that time the boss wife walk on the floor everyone got quiet. Well, is this Penny? She look around at everyone.

Yes ma.

And she smile good job my sister.

And she give me a big rug. Then she went back toward the office.

Everyone stood there in shock.

Some yell this must a dream! Did you see who gave Penny a smile and hug?

Yeah, she did. Danny stood there in shock too. Wow, it must going to thunder and lightning tonight.

That woman don't like nobody. I bet she don't like her shelf. Miss. Berry look at Penny.

Girl, what did you do deserve this? Another employee yell.

I don't know? I guess being myself. And I do whatever get the job done.

Let me go to work before they try take it back. Okay!

Boy, boy, what can I say?

Someone don't want me to leave this place. But I'm tried working for these little pennies. Maybe the boss heard I was leaving here.

And he trying keep me here by making me the employee month. Na, he could've because I haven't told anyone yet.

But that well and good. He isn't talking about giving me a rise. I got find away tell my friend that I got to go.

Hey, how was your weekend? We see you getting in the beautiful car Friday?

Is this your new boyfriend? Danny look up at her.

Na, it just a friend ask me go dinner with him.

I thought I told you guys I don't have time for a man.

But he was cute though. Penny just smile.

Yeah, it was wonderful. We sit down eating some great bar- q. And having clean fun. For once in a long time.

But on that other hand what about you?

Since you all into my business. Penny just smiling.

Oh, sorry you know I can't help myself being noise. Because you my friend that I love so much.

I didn't do much. But help my wife clean up the house. One of her best friend came to visit. And you know how you women do when company come over.

What you mean yawl women? Penny just stare at him.

She wanted the house be cleaned head to toe. I never cleaned up like that before in my life. Danny shake his head.

Danny! What?

Well, my brother she ought to make you clean every weekend. Penny burst out laughing.

I bet you are a lazy man around the house.

You probably laying up trying catch a game on television.

Well, yeah that what we men do.

Now you got it all wrong. She isn't your personal slave. I know you heard the old saying.

What? Danny just stood there.

If you love help me. You shouldn't put all the responsibility on her. At the end of the day she will be too tired spend time with you. All she wanted to go take a shower get dress for bed.

And the Lord God said, (It is) not good that the man should be alone; I will make him an help meet for him.

Therefore shall a man leave his father and his mother, and shall cleave unto his wife: and they shall be on flesh.

Wow, let turn the table. If that was you how you would feel.

Coming home after long day at work.

Then come home have to cook and clean the house. On top that dealing with the kid's drama.

You make a good point. Danny tears roll down his face. Girl, why you had to step on my toes this morning.

I guess, because I love you my brother. Penny gave him a hug.

Now go ahead call that woman. And let her know you sorry. The way you being treated her around the house. And now on you to going help her clean up. You just might get some play tonight.

Okay, my sister.

Well, yes I hope so. Because you're right. That her famous word I'm tired.

And she don't want be bought for years. Okay bye. I got get some work done.

Hey, Paul how your date? Or sorry the interview. Now you trying be funny. It was just an interview. Okay!

But it went well and I hired her.

She supposedly start Monday. Soon she finished her paper work online. And take her drug test and the back ground check. If all that cleared.

Okay, but what that look on your face bro. Hey, what you mean? Rick smiling

Boss who you fooling? You know I know you my brother. And I been around you too long. I see this won't be your last time you will see her.

Yes, right I will see her at work. Paul smile. Bro, you know what I mean.

Well, be honest I hope so. This only one seem so different than the others girl.

Well, yes you just seem her just once.

Boy, you need some patient. Before you run her away.

Okay, you're right. Paul smile.

Well, let me call this girl to see what going on with her. She better answer her phone. I got going give her an ear full of news. What happen other night? I finally found my man. And I can't wait until our first date.

Hey, Penny please call me back. Don't wait three day to call me. I need you call me soon as possible. It important. This is Freedom.

I wondering who calling know I'm at work.

I bet that old Freedom. I just call her back. Soon as I get off work. Because she going to talk me to death. What happen at bible study?

And I got tell her how was my interview. And I got a better job before her.

I hope she don't be jealous.

Penny, girl it lunch time. Let go eat I'm hungry. I hope my wife put something good my box. Danny smiling.

Yea, yea, come on you know lunch go so fast. Penny grab her lunch bag.

So was your weekend? I was very interesting. Penny grab a chair from the next table.

Hey, Penny how are you? Mrs.Larry took her seat.

Girl, I am great. You know they made me the employee of the week. They going give me 100 dollar on my next check.

Wow, that great. Girl I been here almost 20 yr. They never gave me anything but a headache. Every time I ask for a rise they just smile at me. And tell me the company isn't making enough money now right.

Sorry, all rise frosted. Miss. Larry shake head.

I know because I ask them for one too. And they told me the same things. Miss. Charmin.

So I got some new to tell you guys. I have an interview on Friday.

That why I was dress up. What?

Did you get another job? Mrs. Larry had a sad look on her face. The bell rang.

Aw, I got to go to the restroom. Penny drop her head. Because she don't how tell her friends that she leaving.

Sorry, I talk to you later.

What? Why you won't just tell us. Mrs. Larry yell as she clean off the table.

I will, I promise.

Okay, whatever? I hope you have a good day.

Hey, Danny Friday is my last day here. Stop, lying!

Do you remembering asking me Friday why I was dress up? And I told you had some business take care.

Yes, I remembered!

I had an interview from Donald's Law firm. And I got the job. Penny look down.

Girl, that good news. Hold your head up.

Go make that money. We going to be alright.

Well, that mean if I need hold a piece chain. I know who get the money.

If I get the opportunity too. I'm out of here and I won't look back.

Well, for now I'll be here because my baby need a pair shoes. I and Jesus going to work it out.

Aw, thanks Danny for making me feel better.

Hey, if they have an opened please hallow at your boy.

Okay, I will do. Tears roll down his eyes.

In every give thanks: for this is the will of God in Christ Jesus concerning you.

Now, I got tell Ms. Larry too. But I don't know how? I know she will going to be hurt.

Because she was the first person came to me say hello. I use to eat lunch alone. One day I came in the break room she grab my hand.

And she said girl you isn't going eat lunch alone today. You're welcome sit with us. We maybe old women but we love have some company. I never had no one do that for me. Tears running down her face.

Yes, I understand it come a time when you have to leave. Remembered we all here for a seasoning. Now this you're seasoning. Go for it if you make too much money. Just put it an envelope and slide it under my door. I always can use it.

You so funny.

You can always stick your head in the door. Just to say hello sometimes.

Yes, you're right. Danny.

I will tell her before we go home. The bell rang to go home.

Hey, Ms. Larry I have something to tell. Yes, I know she smile.

I'm going to miss you Penny had a sad look on her face. Yes, I already know you found another job.

Hey, how you know I was leaving? I knew it last week.

I had a dream you was enter a big double doors. And I knew we didn't have it here Ms. Larry stood here.

What? Why you didn't tell me?

Because you would believe me. That why I keep until myself. I'm sad but you have my blessing. I'm going to be alright.

But please don't let your success go to your head.

And don't forget about us down here struggles day to day trying make a dollar of 15 cent.

I promise I won't let that happen. Regard you always be my friend. And you have your number. I will be checking time to time you guys. Penny smile

For if a man think himself to be something, when he is nothing, he deceiveth himself.

And please keep me in your prayer. And keep in touch. Oh, I don't have long here either.

What you mean? Miss. Larry

Because I'm getting ready to retired myself. So I can start enjoy life for a change. Instead me working myself to an early grave.

I'm going online hoping a man caught my eyes. I'm getting tried living alone. I had kick my son out the house.

Why? Miss. Larry.

Because he getting to old. And every grown person need their own place. I still love him.

Okay, that right. Girl stand your ground. That what wrong with these kids today. That what my friend dad did to her. She had to go and don't look back.

Wow, that man sound like he mean. Yep!

Don't want turn mommy a loose. Because they won't no responsibility. But they want the benefit.

Yeah, you're right. Penny.

Well, girl give a big hug. I see you in the morning. Yes Ma.

Chapter 13

Who Pimping Who?

Well, I wondering what going with this girl. She won't answer her phone. I guess I got stop by her when I get off work. I hope this time she went food shopping. I know she get pay by now. I just may need a sandwich or two. Instead glass of ice water.

Freedom get ready come back from lunch.

Maybe I will call Peter before I caught this bus later. Maybe he will pick me up.

Na, that isn't going to happen. I think he is playing game with me. Because he gave me his number too fast.

Hey, Freedom why you coming back from lunch later smiling. Miss. Low yelled cross the floor.

I just come from the restroom. Girl, I got my man on my mind Girl, when you found a man?

Yes, I told you I got man two month ago. Well, let me see a picture of him.

Aw, aw, I don't have it in my phone right now. Freedom looking confused.

Okay, Miss. Low walk back to her machine.

Oh, she think she can fool me. Why she don't have at least one picture of him.

Wow, she just call me out. But she right I do need some pictures of him.

Just maybe someone believe me. Freedom drop head she walk back to her machine.

The bell rang to go home.

Come on, girl it time go home. Miss. Low gathered her things. Okay, I'm coming I got catch this bus.

I'm getting tired of this place. Soon I know my man going tell me that I don't have to work anymore.

But I would have you know, that the head of every man is Christ; and the head of the woman is the man; and the head of Christ is God.

Freedom, why are you dreaming? Isn't too many men going to tell their woman quick their job?

Unless they don't have any choice because a situation arrived. They can't solve it. Or their health prevent them too keep working.

Girl, what make you so special?

He must have a good job. Miss. Low getting ready opened the door.

Oh, matter fact what kind of job he have?

Well, it a top secret job. He can't tell me. Freedom knowing she was lying.

Lying lips are abomination to the Lord: but they that deal truly are his delight.

Because she was embarrassed. She really don't know him.

Yea, I better call him. Hoping we can have dinner or something soon. So we get to know one another. She whispered under her breathe.

Bye I see you in the morning. Miss. Low

Boy, I just made a fool out of myself. I got get my story straight.

Good morning, Mr. Britt how are you? Well, I doing alright and I won't complain. And you? Peter.

Oh, I'm okay.

Hey, I did make it to bible study? Yes, I did!

Great? Did you learn something while you there? Mr. Britt smile.

Well, nothing really because I was running late. And I couldn't get my mind together.

That never happen to me. Let me be honest my body was there. But my mind was somewhere else. All I could thinking about finding me a woman.

Peter, you telling me you went the house of the Lord to find you a woman.

Yes Sir, I think I find her. And I think she widow who have money. She said she going to call me. Maybe we can go out to dinner.

Boy, why you allow the devil rob you? That could been your last message. And you allow your private did all the talking for you.

What you mean? Mr. Britt my private. Peter, you know what I mean.

No! Please example yourself.

Your nature!

But I say unto you, That whosoever looketh on a woman to lust after her hath committed adultery with her already in his heart. Oh, I never thought of it like that Peter drop his head.

And another thing you better be careful. Why? Peter getting ready clock in.

Well, she maybe getting ready a pimping. What? Peter burst out laughing.

Yeah, Mr. Britt look over his glasses.

No, way she can't be a pimp. Because she is a woman.

Boy, you don't know nothing. Anyone can be a pimp.

Okay, please tell me what you're talking about? Peter look at him with a funny look on his face.

I know because Kimber (ex-wife) was a pimp too. At first I didn't see it. Until one day my wife stop by my job. She told me she need some money pay a bills.

So I gave her my credit card to her. I didn't think much of it.

One of the guy yell why you allow your wife pimp you?

I shake my head and look up to see who was talking to me. It a huge man smiling at me.

Yes!

Mr. what are you talking about? Why you say wife is a pimp?.

Sorry, I didn't mean any harm. But I couldn't help myself. He walked across the floor.

Okay, please example it.

Oh, I will come find you at lunch. Because I don't have any time right now.

Okay! Thanks

Boy, it was bought me. The man calling my wife a pimp. I couldn't work and waiting for the bell ring for lunch.

What happen next? Peter grab a sandwich from his bag. The bell rang.

I run into the break room. I forgot my lunch. Max, yell come sitting with us fellows.

We going to school you my friend.

Hey, fellow meet my new friend. Hello!

Oh, matter of fact what is your name? Britt and you?

They call me big Max around here. I'm glad to meet you.

Well, let me get back to the subject about. This is how some women work.

Right guy! Yeah

They play this game to see who going take more from the relationship. They look for a nice guy who don't mind do whatever they want. And so they can take advanced of you. By the time you figure out the game you been play.

She would start a big fight with you.

So it will give her away out the relationship or marriage. And she will try blame you for the break up. Having your head all mess up.

And you wondering what you did to cause it. In reality she didn't really love you. But the things you can do for her. Tears run down my face.

Yes, it still hurt. It been over 8 years ago. I pour out my heart. Because she stole my heart the first time I saw her.

Boy, he mess up my head.

Then I went home thinking what Max said.

When I found out he was true my wife was taking my money. To go see another man and buying him things. She found online. And I find out he was a younger man then me.

All she wanted me take care of her. While she was entertain someone else in jail.

I wanted kill her but I had to pray that things off of me. Before I be sitting in jail beside him for murder.

I just help her pack her bag. And took the near hotel.

I went even further I pay for one night. Because I know God going take care of it.

And he did! The last time I heard she is having problem after problem. And the guy still lock down.

Be not deceived; God is not mocked: for whatsoever a man soweth, that shall he also reap.

Peter got quit because he trying be sometime he isn't also. Yeah, that my story. Don't let your story end up like mine. Because you didn't see coming.

Okay, Mr. Britt

I got to go now.

Well, let jump on the bus to see what this girl up to. And why she haven't return my phone call.

Wow, I'm getting hungry all suddenly. I guess those two sandwich I ate early wasn't enough. Because my stomach is talking to me.

F. e. e. d m .e! Freedom grab her things getting on the bus.

Let me try call her. Let her know I'm on my way to her house. And tell her get rid the ice water. Because I want something to eat.

Girl, why won't you answer your phone. If you isn't going to answered your phone. Stop paying the bill.

I finally made it to her house. Now she better be home. I had to catch two buses to get here. I already upset. And I have wait on the next bus.

I knock on her door like the policeman. I bet this might get her attend.

Who, is it? Penny jump out the shower. It is me, Freedom let me in.

Girl, wait a minute let grab something put on. I was in the shower.

Okay, because I don't want see all your goodness anyway. Who that man you try put out the side door? Freedom yell. Girl, I know you lost your mind. Come in before woke up my neighed. Then they going to stick their head out of the door. Penny whispered.

Okay, I know how to solve that problem. Freedom smiling. Girl, I don't want hear.

All you need to do when your neighed stick their head of the door again. Just flash them. They will get their eyes full they won't be peeking no more.

No way, in the name of Jesus.

I may not able get rid these old men. Peeking in my window. And they be waiting outside for me come home from work.

Now I know for sure you are c r a z y. Penny just shake her head. Well, why you haven't answered my calls?

Sorry, but you know this girl have to work too.

Okay, I understand all that but you could've text me.

Yep, but I have some good news.

Okay please tell me but wait a minute I need to make me a sandwich first.

Girl, why you always come on my house hungry? And you don't never bring me something to eat.

You know I don't have it like that. Freedom smile

You just got lucky I have some peanut butter and crackers on the counter. You can have a glass of ice water too. Please help yourself.

Penny burst out laughing.

Why you playing with me? You know I don't care for it. But you said you hungry.

Now, you want acting funny. Never mind I wait stop by mom house. Maybe she cook but I have to hear daddy mouth. Saying why I haven't buy some food put in my house.

So you won't have to come over here bagging for our bread. And be he alright.

Girl, just shout up you always got a smart comment.

Na, I just tell you the truth. I know the truth hurt sometimes. Freedom look at her.

And you shall know the truth, and the truth shall make you free. Well anyway, I got tell this news

Okay, okay, let me have it. I better take a seat. I know it going to be something crazy.

See that why I don't tell you everything.

Girl, stop lying go ahead before I fall asleep.

Do you remember I told you I was going to bible study?

Yeah! Because I told you don't think about asking me to go with you.

See I told you always have smart comment. Penny No, I'm not lying

Guess, who sat by me? Jesus!

No, stop playing Penny. He will never forsake you.

My man his name Peter. And he ask me for my number. Okay, did you give it to him?

No, but I ask him for his number.

I supposedly call maybe set up a date. Well, did call him yet?

No, I been busy. What?

Freedom, what was so important you did call him? And that all you use to talk about.

I want to know Penny lay across the bed.

Be honest I don't know.

I guess, I'm afraid what might happen.

Fool, oh I'm sorry. I didn't mean to call you that.

Girl, why you scared now?

What about the house on the hill, the beautiful car. And buy the wigs you wear different one every day of the week. Penny sit back in her chair.

Okay, I will call him tomorrow. To see what up too.

Now, what new you dying to tell me?

Oh, do you remember you ask me why I couldn't we hang out last Friday. And I told you I had sometimes do.

Yeah! I went home got in bed. I had an interview.

What? Penny are you for real? Yeah, Freedom.

So what happen? Did you have the job? What kind of job it is?

Hey, wait a minute let me finished. I will tell you everything.

Freedom, I see you don't have no patient. Yeah, I know!

I start my new job next Monday. What? Freedom stood up.

Oh, I be working for a law firm.

Girlfriend, what you know about the law? Nothing, yet but I can learned. Penny smile.

Yeah, right they going make you their personal goof. I hope you have some good running shoes.

Why? I have all type of shoes in my closet.

Good, they going to having you go get their mail. You better learn fast how to make some coffee.

What you mean? Freedom you love my coffee.

No, I don't I just drink it. Because I really don't have a choice. Oh, it like that!

Yeah, when you are cold. You will drink anything to get warm.

Girl, your coffee taste like mud. Sorry I don't want hurt your feeling.

Well, let me teach you.

I don't want get fired on your first day. Do yourself a favor. Okay, Penny.

If they ask you make them some coffee. You better hope it a Starbucks close.

Why?

Go buy it there! They won't know the difference. Girl, you must be crazy Freedom.

I am isn't going to do it.

Well, okay you better pray they don't run of toilet paper. You going to be in trouble.

What you mean? Penny with a strange look on her face.

The office going smell be like a shrink have spray up in there. Freedom, you so nasty!

What?

Go home! You can spoil a good dream.

Don't hate on a sister. I thought you going be glad for me. Yes, I am. See I'm smiling.

Yeah, I better go home. I can't get nothing to eat.

It time me run over to mom house see what she cook. Girl, I talk you later. Freedom give her a hug.

Hey, don't trying call me after 9.00 clock. I'm going be in bed try catch up my rest.

Oh Yep, you're right. I see those bags under your eyes.

Girl, shout up! I saw you with that old wig off your head. And it don't like pretty.

Since you want to go there. Penny shaking head she while opened the door.

Oh, you putting me out now.

Yeah, you already stay little long too. Go worry someone else for a while. But I love you.

Okay, I know you don't love me anymore. Why? Penny stood in the door.

You don't keep no food up in here for me. Hold up, you want me get like my grandma.

Did you forget the time last I was over your house? You didn't have nothing here but brown banana. I hope you don't think somebody won't to eat them. Penny still standing in the door.

Who? Freedom put her on her hip. Your roaches!

Bye!

Chapter

It Finally Happen

Well, I did promise Peter I will call him.

Maybe I call him when I get home. Freedom whisper toherself.

Now I can get into the shower now.

It been a long day. Penny getting herself together.

By that time she walk in the bathroom. Her phone rang.

Oh, no it better not be Freedom calling me. I'm not going to answer it right now. I'm going to soak my tired my body for a while.

Little she knew it was Paul calling her. Just to remember her. She got to come in the morning. Because she have to finish up some paper and go take a drug test.

She let it to went to vocal mail.

Hey, Miss. Penny I just call you let you know I need you to come in the morning. Finished up your paper work.Don't forget bring your I.d and your birthcertificate also.

I hope didn't disturb you.

Wow, that sound like Paul vocal. When that man speak something go all over my body.

Lord, let me stop thinking that way about that man. He going be my boss pretty soon. I don't want him get anymore idea.

Lord, he is different from the other guys I dated and fine too. Please forgive me I'm just human. Sometimes I let me motion run wild.

Sitting here in this big house I'm getting alone. And I wishing I had someone share it with me.

Let me get out this shower put on some clothes. And run to the store buy me something for dinner tonight.

Penny whisper to herself.

I better grab my phone to see who was calling me early. Oh, I was right it was Paul.

I wondered should I call him back or not. It getting later he may be busy or with his family.

Well, if I don't call him back. He may think I'm isn't interest in the job. And he find will someone else. Penny debating.

Okay, I'm going call him.

His phone just rang and rang.

I knew that was a bad idea. Let me go in the store before it get crowded.

Well, what look good to eat? I think I will find something quick cook. Maybe a freezer dinner be great.

Well, I better stop by the grocery store. Before go home because Doug don't have nothing in the house to eat. But some old milk and it out dated. So I won't drink that. Maybe I grab something quick to eat.

And I get something for my lunch for tomorrow. Peter thinking to herself.

Ask Penny walk around the corner she run into Peter. Knocking his things out of his hands.

Oh, I so sorry Paul. I will pick it up.

Hey my sister, my name isn't Paul you got the wrong guy

Well, I'm very sorry. As she gathered his things he walk away. He didn't say anything.

Wow, I'm wondering why Paul acting like that. Maybe he don't won't no one know he knew me.

Or then again maybe he having a bad day.

I wondered why this woman call me Paul. When my name is Peter.

I hope there isn't any one look like me. Get me into some trouble.

Little Penny knew she run into Peter. Paul twin brother. Which neither brother don't know it.

Now, that got me thinking if I come to work for the company. I wondered if he going act like that toward me. Or he going be rude to me. But I did try apologize to him. Maybe I need think twice about this job. I don't want make big mistake working for someone like that. Just mean to everyone he contact with.

Then I can't go back my current job.

Yeah, I better pray hard before I jump into something

I may regret lately.

Wow, I can't tell Freedom what just happen to me.

She would love hear some juicy news about me. I can hear her running her mouth.

Saying Girl, everything sound good don't mean it true. And you better not take that job. Just keep what you already have.

Because you already know you can handle it. Then go into something you don't know nothing about.

I must finished what I started that way. I won't be wondering if I should've or not took the job. I know what I will do. I just take off a few days. If I don't like it I still have my job. I can't afford just jump up quick my job. And I don't know if this what I want. Then I'll have to accept it because I got the pay bills. And I hate it.

The way of a fool is right in his own eyes: but he that hearkeneth unto counsel is wise.

Freedom, jump on the bus.

Man, I tried riding this bus with all these noise people. And it started smelling bad on here. Maybe I should be like Penny get me another job. So I can buy me a car even though I can't drive.

Hey, Mr. bus driver this is my stop. Okay, you have good night ma.

Thanks, you do the same.

As I walking off the bus.

There was Paul walking out the store with a lady and some kids. But Freedom thought it was Peter. But it was Paul and her sister. Yet she don't have any clue they are identify twins.

No it can't be truth, Peter lie to me. He said he was single. Tears roll down her face.

I was going to call him soon I got home tonight. Why, Lord this man got a woman and have kids.

Why he didn't waited on me? But I don't know about having kids.

My patient is too short. And they just be in my way. We won't have time for each other's. Because I be at home with the kids. While he at work probably he don't want come to a noisy home.

What I'm going to do now? I already told Penny that me and Peter going out a date.

I can hear her mouth. I told you so. That man maybe marriage. And stop running behind him man.

Just wait on the Lord send you someone. Instead you trying to do it yourself. Why you keep running into dead end wall?

Delight thyself also in the Lord; and he shall give thee the desires of thine heart. The steps of a good man are ordered by the Lord; and he delighteth in his way.

Oh, I know what I'm going to do? I'm going to keep pretending everything okay.

So I better call him just see what going really on with him. And find out who that woman is. I just might have to put a little bug in her ear. It time to move on my sister. I'm claiming this piece of meat. I will allow him pay the child support. Because that his responsibly. Everything else going to be mine.

Wow, Don (sis) look over there that woman staring us. Where? Sis

Over to your left she just got off the bus. Oh yeah, now I see her.

Hey, don't point at her. She may know who I am and try rob us. Let me grab these kids by their hands.

Okay, okay! Sis started walking fast to the car.

And don't looking back. She will know we're watching her. Wow, that was a close one. Paul hurry put the kids in the car. Boy, she just might a stalker.

Freedom finally made it to her mother house.

I hope this old dog sleep. Every times I come over visit he always barking. Waking up the neighborhood.

Mr. Tut run out the house half dress with his bat in his hand. Thinking someone trying rob him.

Boy, that naughty.

I hope mom isn't already gone to bed. I know dad don't go to bed until the sun rise.

And I matter well get ready hear his mouth.

Why you don't buy some food put in your house? Well, here I go.

I wondering who knocking at my door this time of the night. It better not be the police. I don't know nothing and I haven't saw nothing. Because isn't my business.

Boy, they know how mess up a good night up.

Let me get myself up to see who keep knocking at my door. Who is?

We all sleep. He yelled.

Dad, how you sleep you're talking to me. Oh, is this Freedom?

Yes, dad.

What you want? Why you always come around here this time of the night.

Well, Dad I guess I miss you.

Stop lying! Try that again. No, that isn't good enough for me opened my door.

Dad, stop play open this door. Before that old dog start barking. I don't want Mr. Tut come out you know that man is naughty. His belly hanging down with all that hair on it.

Girl, bring your behind in. But wait!

Dad, what wrong with you? Freedom look around. I'm isn't trying to rob you.

Well, I know that. Because you won't get nothing but some bundle of bills. That I and your mother owe you're welcome to pay them.

I know your mother will appreciate it. Yea, I know!

Where mom?

Girl, you know your mom already in the bed sleep. Lately, that all she want to do.

Well, I think she get tired of my mouth. Dad, what you mean? Your mouth.

This house is a mess.

Yea, dad you're right. But who made this mess? Me!

Well, dad you answered your on question.

Well, what you mean? And what you trying to say? Oh, now I know why mom always in the room.

She wait on you clean up this naughty house. And I don't blame her.

Little girl, you better watch your mouth. Before you be picking yourself off this floor.

Sorry, Daddy.

That a woman job. She supposed to clean up this house.

Because I'm the head of this castle.

If she didn't read the fine print. Before she marriage me that her bad luck.

Dad! What?

Why you so mean? I can't help myself.

But mom taught us girls while you was at work. We isn't a man foot spool. But we are our help mate.

And the Lord God said, It is not good that man should be alone; I will make him an help meet for him.

And the rib, which the Lord God had taken from man, made he a woman, and brought her unto the man.

Therefore shall a man leave his father and his mother, and shall cleave unto his wife: and they shall be one flesh.

Now see daddy that mean you supposedly share everything together with mom.

So dad you matter well get ready pull your sleeve up. Jump on this broom and ride it.

Maybe mom come out of the room.

Girl, I should knew your mother up to something.

Yea, that my mom for you. Freedom burst out laughing. This isn't funny!

Yea is it! Because you made the mess you should've cleaned it up.

Go home!

Yea, I think my time up.

But dad, wait a minute did mom cook today. Yes! But you can't have any.

I should knew why you come over here. To get you a plate. The kitchen is close for tonight. Unless you want to grab that broom and you ride it for me.

No fair dad you think you smart. I'm not trying do your dirty work.

Yea!

Well, sorry that isn't going to happen. Freedom reaching for a plate.

Girl, how many time I told you didn't bring a bag in. What make you think you can carry out a bag out?

Dad, stop tripping let me have something to eat. I said no!

You isn't going let your favor girl go hungry. Yea!

I am tired of you think you can take my food out of the house.

Oh, dad now you woke up mom. I know mom going to give it to me.

Now, look what you made me do. I can hear her tripping get this house clean up. Before the church ladies come over for prayer tomorrow.

Well, dad what you wait on? Freedom burst out laughing. Bye, daddy you have good night. While you cleaning up.

Girl, give me a hug you looking like your mommy. Freedom still laughing.

Hey, don't let your laugh catch up with you. Okay daddy, I love you.

Chapter 15

This Can't Be True

I hope this bus don't take all night to get here. Well, let me call this man to see what up too. Hey, is this Peter?

Yes, this me! Who speaking?

My name is Freedom. We met at church last Tuesday night doing bible study.

Oh yea, now I remembered you. Yes, I just call to see what you doing?

Well, I just finished dinner. Peter smile. Okay! Did you save me some your dinner?

Sure, I can make you a turkey sandwich.

Oh, okay! Well that sounds good. But you forgot the potato chip on the side,a big pickle And big red soda.

Aw man, that would've been great with it. Why I didn't think of it.

Freedom started thinking to herself. Why this man supposedly have a woman eating a cold cut.

Hey, I see you today when I was getting off the bus early. Na, you couldn't have saw me because I came straight home from work. Trying to catch the mail truck. Because I had a package should've been here by now. I didn't want it sit outside my door too long.

People up here take your stuff and sale it.

Oh, really sorry! Well, you must have a twin out here. No, I don't. I have a sister they say we look alike.

Okay, do your sister have kids?

Oh, she don't have a child yet. But she pregnant this her first child.

Sorry, my eyes must playing trick on me. Peter burst out laughing.

Where you get that phrase from? Oh yea!

Now I'm confused I know what my eyes saw.

I think this man lying to me. He don't want me to know that he is marriage. And have kids too. But I will play alone with his game. Until I find out the true. Freedom thought to herself.

Wow, I wondered why she said that. Well, they us to say tell me that we have everyone look like us.

Oh, I remember I was younger my friends trying ague with me. That they saw me at a football game one Friday night.

But, I know I was at my mother house at that time. Now here she saying the same thing.

Well, if that true I pray he don't do something get me into trouble.

Hey, are you free Saturday night?

Maybe why? Freedom had a smile on her face.

I thought if you want get to know me. You take me out for dinner.

E. x. c .u. s. e M. e?

While a minute I thought the man supposedly peruse a woman. Not the other way around the woman chasing the man.

Whoso findeth a wife a good thing, and obtaineth favour of the Lord.

Okay, now you can ask me out. Just maybe I would think about it.

Oh, really it like that! You playing hard to catch. Yeah, Freedom burst out laugh.

Hey, what so funny?

You! Freedom getting on the bus.

Peter if that your real name. Why you so shy just a girl out.

Well, I think she going say yes. Now what time you want this girl to be ready.

Are you going to pick up this girl? Or you going to make her catch the bus.

Okay, I will pick up you. Just text me your address.

I better call Penny tell her about this. She may fall out of her bed.

Aw, man my phone dead. I forget to charge my phone. When I was over dad.

Boy, dad make you lose your mind fooling around with him. I guess I will call her in the morning.

The alarm went off.

Penny jump out the bed and run into the shower. Her phone rang.

Why Lord, someone calling me this early?

Can I wake up first and get a little coffee in me first? It better not be Freedom.

I'm tired of her talking about this man. She need leave that alone before she get her feeling hurt again.

Well, let me put on some clothes. So I can get my day started. And check this phone when I finished dressing. To see who calling me this early.

It was the law firm.

I wondering what they wanted.

I know I supposedly be there at 8 this morning.

I hope Paul haven't change his mind. And he had put someone else in my place.

Because I may not be able go back to my job.

I know the boss heard I found another job.

Lord, should I call them back. Or wait go in get my feeling hurt. Penny heart pumping fast.

I hate go there they turn me around at the door. So I better make this called.

Hello, is this Donald Law's firm. Yes!

Maybe help you Ma?

Yes, my name is Penny Louis. I supposed to come in this morning.

Okay, Ma. So what the problem?

Oh, I just wondering I got a phone from you guys.

Yes, that was Mr. Paul calling see to if change your mind. Or needed a ride.

Oh, no I haven't change my mind. I be there soon the bus run. Okay, thanks I see later.

Little she know when she walk out her door. Paul sitting outside waiting on her.

Penny hurry up put on her shoes and grab her things. Ran out the door their Paul waiting with some flower.

Penny was speechless. Her mouth opened but no word come out.

Oh, why you at house?

I'm sorry I was in the neighborhood. And I thought would give you a ride to work.

Hey, wait a minute how you found my house.

Oh, it call goggle map. Plus your address on your application Paul smile.

Wow, why I didn't think of it. Penny shake her head.

Well, can I give you a ride?

Oh, yeah I save my 2.00 dollar for the bus. When I go home later. Okay! Paul smile.

Wow, you have nice car. They must pay you great. Thanks! It okay.

Someday I will have me a car too. I'm tired riding the old bus. But I'm isn't trying complained.

I thank God for it because I couldn't survive without it. I'm isn't the only one a lot others in my shoes too.

Depend on it.

Not that I speak in respect of want; for I have learned, in whatsoever state I am, therewith to be content.

Yes, I understand.

Well, we here. Paul smile.

Hey, do me a favor don't let anyone know I gave you a ride. Okay, my mouth is seal. I'm just thankful for the ride Penny smiling.

Wow, I got tell Freedom about this. Soon I get a break. Well, let me get up these tall stairs.

Boy, I wasn't trying get a work out this morning. But I got do what a sister got to do.

I finally made up the stairs. I stop catch my breath. I didn't know I was out of shape like this. Maybe I do need join somebody gym soon.

And I matter well make Freedom join me. It won't hurt her just tone up the fat around her neck.

I can't be feeling like this every morning. Because I don't know what they going having me to do.

I walk in the big double door. It almost knock me down.

A lady standing in the lobby. Welcome, to Donald's Law firm. You must be Miss. Penny Lewis.

Yes!

I heard a lot about you. The lady smile come on with me. Okay, I hope Mr. Paul say something nice about me. Penny smile.

Yes, he did.

Oh, I'm sorry my name Gail the sectary. If need anything I will take care of it.

Okay, thanks

Oh, I need you take a seat over here. I need your I.D. And your birth certificate. So I can put it your file. While I'm making a copy of them. I have two short video you must watch first. Then after you finished it. You will take the test. It going to show us you're weak and your strong area.

So we don't want put you somewhere you can't handle. Okay, Penny smile while she took off her coat.

By that time Paul walk in the office.

Good morning, Gail how are you doing? Oh, I am fine.

Miss. Penny is here.

Oh, okay great! Send her in my office when she finished her paperwork.

Paul walk back in his office.

Hey, Paul want to see when you finished. Okay, she smile.

Let me start focus before I take this test.

I got past this test. Because I can't afford be sitting out door.

Hey, after you finished. I need you go to the restroom for a drug test. Don't take anything with you. Do you need a bottle water to help you? Gail smile

Na, I think I can handle it. But thanks.

By that time her phone rang.

I know this better not be Freedom calling.

I don't have the time talk to her. I told her I'm going to the law firm this morning. I wondered what part did she forgot.

Let me see who call me. I got to watch this video. Yep, it was her.

Girl, answered your phone. I got a lot of things to tell you. But it went to her voice mail.

Well, never mind I call back at lunch time.

I better get my mind in the building. Before I will be looking for another job.

Boy, I just can't believe Peter would lie to me. I will get to the bottom of this.

Good morning Freedom, why you talking to yourself? Oh, Freedom turn around.

I don't know? I guess I'm in love with myself.

Okay, please don't answer yourself. People going to think you're C. r .A. z. Y. Hazel smile.

Girl, I am! Didn't you know? No!

Hazel look at me with stranger look on her face. You see no one in here bought me.

And you have a good morning. I went to clock in. I bet you will leave me alone now.

Let me try again call this girl. She better answer the phone.

But it went to her voice mail again. Okay, I give up. Let me get in here grab me a cup coffee. Before the bell rang.

Hey, Mr. Britt I think I got a dinner date. Oh, yeah good morning Peter.

Oh I'm sorry good morning.

How you manger do that? Mr. Britt stood outside the break room door.

 Well, I didn't do nothing.

What you mean? Did you have buy some candy or flowers? No, do you remembered I was telling about the lady.

I met in church. I gave her my number but she didn't me her.

Yes, I remembered. I thought that was strange.

Oh she call me last night. But she think I have a wife and kids. And she accuse me that she saw me with a woman and some child. Peter smile.

Man, what you have done now?

Mr. Britt I haven't done anything. And I don't have a woman or any kids. I believe someone trying me setting up.

Okay, don't let your past come back hunt you. Oh, you don't believe me?

Well, isn't for me to believe you better hope that woman find out the truth.

Oh okay!

Man, you maybe you have twin out there.

I hope not he can mess me up with the ladies.

There you go again trying be playboy.

I told you leave those women alone. Before they mess you up. Before you end up like Samson. Delilah mess up him.

Samson was so strong no one couldn't defend him. And he was a hero of Israelites. The Philistines wanted to know his secret how they can defend him. When they found out his bigger weakness was a woman.

The Philistines use a woman name Delilah. To find out what was Samson secret. And she did it was his hair. She cut his hair.

She mess him up. The Philistines defend him. Now you see how a woman can mess you for life.

The bell rang.

Yeah, it time Peter yearning. I talk to you later my friend.

Yeah, yeah, I better pray for you. Mr. Britt turn around and smile.

Oh, please do! I will find this person look like me. And so I can tell please don't mess up game.

Boy, you need help go work.

The bell rang it break time.

Excuse me, ma could you tell me where the break room. Penny smile

Oh, sure you must be new. Yes, ma! I just started today.

Okay, glad to see a new face around here. Oh, sorry my name is Miles

Okay, I'm glad to meet you. My name is Penny.

Oh, yea that an odd name. I bet your daddy name you .Miles smile

No, my mother did?

Okay, just follow me. I'm going there myself. I need me a strong cup of coffee without sugar.

Do you want some too? Miles opened the door. Oh no, I can't drink coffee. It make me shake.

But thanks anyway Penny smile. Wow, this big break room.

Yea!

My old break room so small if ten people in it at once. That be to crowd it.

What? I know you joking.

No, and it have a credit card machine too. Penny was so amazing how big this break room.

Girl, where did you worked before came here?

In an old factory. Everything in there so old it seem like every other day. They had to work the on machine. We was more down then we was running.

In the summer time it so hot in it. You could fried an eggs on the machine. And in the winter it just as worth. You better put on three layer of clothes. Or you freeze to death because they keep the opened the door. Because of the truck coming in and out.

Wow! I don't think couldn't handle that. I don't like the cold. Miles shake your head.

Excuse me, I need to call my friend. Let her know how things going with me.

Okay, I need to warm my food up. Before the rang. I hope she still on her lunch break.

Girl, I got some hot news for her ears.

Penny finally call Freedom back.

Hey, I tried three times try calling and still no response. Girl, I was busy. I had to finished some paperwork.

Okay, but you had me worry about thinking something happen to you.

Girl, I didn't know you feel that way about me.

Because we always auger and fuss about something all the time. Yeah, just because we love you each other.

Girl, don't having me crying up in here. Penny wipe her face. Sorry!

In front my new co- worker. Oh how the new job going?

Great! I'm loving it so far.

I'm sitting in this big beautiful break room it almost biggest your house Freedom.

Oh, you for real. Yeah!

They have television on the wall, all type vendor machine, and computers.

Oh, I forgot they have a teller machine. You can charge it. Well sister!

What? Penny look at the phone.

You can't use it. Because you don't own a credit card. Girl, why you hating on me? Freedom.

I know that. But soon I will have one. Then I'm going to flash it in your face. And say how you like me now?

This girl moving on up. Penny rolling her head.

Wow, I need to put my application in too. Maybe they will hire me.

Oh, no Freedom please don't do that. Why?

We both get fried?

You be up here flirting with these guys up in here. And their wives find out. They be up in here ready to kill both of us. Plus I just got this job. And I'm isn't trying to be homeless fooling with you.

But girl, we can riding be in the finest cars. And eat at best restaurant money can buy.

I know they got big bank. And I don't have any problem helping them spend some of it too.

Freedom, you going nuts.

Do you a banana? Come down your nerves.

No, I will looking out for a sister too. But I got get my first. If you know what I mean.

Girl, I don't need to do all that. In a few months I just might have the same.

By doing it the honest way. I'm isn't trying use nobody just trying look good. It come with a price. I'm isn't trying pay the cost.

You better stop before you jump into something you can't handle.

Penny, stop worry so much about me nothing going to happen to me. I'm a big girl. I can take of care myself.

Okay, my sister.

I hope your mother have some bury insurance on you. They just might be able take vacation on you. After they collect the money.

Oh you have joke.

No, Freedom you like playing these danger game.

Some of men don't mind whip your behind. For with their money.

What good will it be for someone to gain the whole world, yet forfeit their soul? Or what can someone give in exchange for their soul?

Bye, girl let me finished my lunch. Before the bell rang. Hey, I will drop by your house. When you off work tonight.

Penny, you better have me something to eat. You already know I'm going be hungry.

Maybe I have something for you. You better pray I get paid today. If not you going be holding your belly again.

No, I'm not you stop playing with me. I have some juicy news to tell. Please answer your phone. If you going to be late. So I can hide from your neighbor.

Oh, what neighbor?

Penny, you know what who I'm talking about. No, I don't!

The old man live across the street from you. He always run outside flashing every one.

The last time I was over you house. He ran up me to flash me holding his bat. He sacred me I almost pee on myself.

I'm not to going let that happen again. (Laughing)

Girl, that wasn't funny.

I can't help myself. I can see you walking down the street with a wet spot in your pant.

Penny! What?

Now that would be nasty.

Girl, just shut up! I don't want think about it. Bye!

Don't be late you know it getting cold at night. And I don't want be standing around too long. Because you have a to many crazy neighbors. They might think I'm trying rob them.

Yeah, I can see it now they hit you all upside your head. You running in the house with knots all over your body.

Penny, don't wish that bad luck on me.

Okay, okay but you already know. I have to take a picture of it. If that happen.

No, that isn't going to happen. So you forget about it. Hey, hey, my supervisor just walk in the door.

I talk to you later girl. I got to go.

Okay, but like I said please don't be late.

Bye, Girl he walking toward me.

Hey how are you? Paul stood front of the table.

Well, let see it better than my other job. Less stressful and it is a clean environment. So far people nicer here. Penny smile.

Okay, great did you finished up your paper work?

No, because the bell rang for break. Miss. Gail told me take a break. I could come back finish up. Plus I have to take a drug test next. I think that all I have to do.

Okay, I will tell Gail when you finished I want to see you.

So I give you a tour of this place. Give you your personal work place. So I can keep you close to me. I want to train you in couple months.

You be ready be on your own.

Wow, you will do that for me. Penny had tears in her eyes. Yes! Why, you crying?

You just don't know no one never take time out for me. I'm so appreciate. And thanking God for giving a chance to prove myself.

Okay, I'm just doing my job. And we can't afford miss train anyone. Because our name stand for excellent Paul smile. Why you smiling?

I knew something different about you. Okay, but what you mean?

How you isn't shame acknowledge God first.

The other ladies around here always talking about their self or others people.

But seek ye first the kingdom of God, and his righteousness; and all these things shall be added unto you.

May, I sit down for a minute with you? Don't worry if the bell ring. I will take care of you.

Sure!

Can I tell you a little secret about me? Yes, I love secret.

Okay, before I come into the doors in the morning. I pray. And after I leave for the day also.

If ye abide in me, and my words abide in you, ye shall ask what ye will, and it shall be done unto you.

What?

Yeah, that why I always have a good day.

Me too. And I try not let nothing get me down.

Because I know God provider.

Oh, you mean Jehovah Jireh. Penny smile. Yeah!

My mother taught us when was a kids. Some of God's names. And she always ask me did I pray today.

Yeah, that woman always praying about something. I think she be praying in her sleep. My dad knows he better not mess with her. She always tell him she going tell her father on him.

If he start acting up. And she be having a serious look on her face too.

You so silly Paul burst out laughing. Yeah, but that is the truth.

Well, we have something in comments. Yea, we both believe God.

Why, everyone looking at me? When they walking out. Oh, because they see a new face around here. Give it a couple week you won't notice it.

They will think you are just one of the girls. Okay, Mr. Paul.

Well, I better get back to work. This my first day I got look good in front of the boss.

Paul, burst out laughing.

Hey, why you laughing? Yeah, that what we do. Okay! You have good day. Thanks!

Paul walk out the break room smiling. I'm the boss. He whispered under his breath.

Hey, wait on me please this place too big. I'm don't want get lost.

Penny grabbing her things rushing out the door. Okay, Paul look back and smile.

Everybody started whispered. I believe the boss may found the one.

Girl, he better not pick her. I been waiting for a long time. And he never look at like me. The way he is looking at her. Are you serious? Susan

Yeah, what wrong with me? She roll her head.

Nothing, but girl have look in the mirror lately? Yes, Mrs. Parker!

I see the same person that I see every morning. Okay!

Now that your problem. Thinking you look good. since no one told you truth.

Well, today is your lucky day. I'm going tell you the truth. What your mother should've told you already.

Maybe she didn't want hurt your feeling.

Mrs. Parker what you talking about? I don't understand.

Yes, I know Because you always look the same every day. You don't wear makeup and some lip stick.

You looking like something die in a movie. And you still wearing those clothes from 1999. It time to clean out your closet. Then maybe some of these men might look at you for a change. Miss. Parker shaking her head.

Okay, I am going home tonight throw everything away. Monday, I will look better then Foxy Brown. Thanks for the advice Susan smile.

Sorry, I should've told you long time ago. Just maybe you would had a man by now.

It okay, I glad you told me.

Girl, let get out this break room. Before we get into trouble.

Paul just smile while he walking down the hall. Hey, why you still smiling?

I'm just enjoying the company.

Okay, well me too.

Well, what you bring for lunch? Paul look down at her.

Well, nothing really something I didn't want to eat. But something better than nothing. I really don't had a chose. Either go hungry all day. Because this sister don't have it right now.

Penny look up Okay, I got you. What you mean?

But please don't tell no one about this. I won't heard the last of it.

Aw thanks, I owe you.

What? Paul look at her with a stranger look.

I meant to say I owe you a dinner for looking out for me. Oh, really! You can cook?

Yeah, I wouldn't be like looking this. Fine then wine. Sorry, I didn't mean to hurt you feeling.

Na, I'm fine. When I do cook that dinner. I'm going to take a picture of you. When lick your fingers.

And you going to tell me it was good with a smile on your face. I bet you!

Paul look at her as they walking down the hall.

Yeah, but you got wait for this sister get paid. Penny stop put her hands on her hip.

Okay, I accept. I haven't had a home cook meal in a long time. Oh, really what about your lady friend.

No, I don't have one. I am single. I thought I told you this before. Is this a trick question Paul smile.

No! Sorry!

Well, me too but I'm isn't look. Okay! Me either.

I got to go now. I will leave a card with the Gail in the office. Just stop by there and pick up. You can buy whatever you want to eat out of the break room. Until you get paid.

What? Are you for real? Yes!

Aw, thanks. Tears roll down Penny face. What wrong now?

Like I say before I never had no one be so nice to me like you. I just doing my Christian duty. Paul smile.

Are you going to stop bye.

Na, I better not. I don't want these women be looking up side your head.

What you mean? Penny burst out laughing.

Most of these women trying got a date with me. It isn't happen because work and pleasure don't mix. When you working to close together.

Okay, I understand.

Well, Mrs. Penny I will talk to you later. Here the office Miss. Gail will take care of you.

Thanks. Paul throw his hand in the air and wave. As he walk back down the hall.

Boy, I can't wait to tell Freedom all about my day.

Well, let me got my head back on work before mess something up. I know I need this job. Maybe one day I'll have a parking space too. Penny smile as she went back in the office.

Hey, Penny! Yes, Ma

We need to finish up this test. And tomorrow you going to start your training.

How to use the computer and how file some papers away. Miss. Gail smile.

Well, not really but I'm ready to learn. This is better than my other job. At least I will go back home cleaned.

Oh yea, I will take good care of you.

Aw, thanks. Penny smile and whisper thank God for favor. Boy, I got a lot to tell Freedom tonight. And how Paul being so good to me. I hope she is having a good day also.

Well, let me get my mind off of her. And finished this test. I can't afford mess this up.

Chapter 16

Who You Fooling

Finally, the ring to go home. Hey Mrs. Penny!
I wondered who calling me. I turn around it Paul waving. So I wave back getting ready walk around to the clock.

Hey, I think you going to need those books. So that you can know the rules and policies. And show how you file away different documents.

Okay, thanks.

Hey, why these books so big? It going take me years to read all of them.

Paul, burst out laughing.

Girlfriend, take long as you need too. I know because it took me a long to write it.

You, said what? Penny look up at him.

Oh, meant the company management took years to write them. Oh, Paul almost blow his cover.

And why you call me girlfriend? Penny stood there waiting for an answered.

Hey, I sorry!

It okay, but please call me Penny. You may say that too long. It could come true.

Oh, wow I never thought it like that.

Yes, do you remember when God called resist things six in day? Penny smile.

Yes, that in the book of Genesis.

Now you seeing the big picture. Penny walking close to the door.

Hold on, what you mean? I'm confused.

Okay, can I break it down? Sure! Paul smiles

God created the heaven and earth?

Yes, that true. Go on. Paul just stood there. Now he give us the same power.

But you got to believe it when you speak it. Oh, you talking about the book of Matthews. Yep!

And Jesus said unto them, Because of your unbelief: for verily I say unto you, If ye have faith as a grain of mustard seed, ye shall say unto this mountain,

Remove hence; to yonder place; and it shall remove; and nothing shall be impossible unto you.

Wow, you know your bible. Penny Yes, if you had mother like mine.

Oh, you going to bible study. No matter what if it was school night. She didn't care. And she use to say if you can give your times to other things, in this house you will give God some of time also.

If you like it or not. So tell your friends don't think about calling you on church night. Or come over visit they will have to go with you.

And she would tell anybody as for me and my house, we will serve the Lord.

Oh, wow your mother sound like mine. She would say the same thing. Penny burst out laughing

So, that mean I should keep calling you girlfriend. Maybe you become mine.

I dared you! Penny stood back. Oh, I just joking with you.

Let me go home. I hope this bus haven't left me. Because, I can't carry all these books walking home.

Oh, I'm sorry I kept you here this long. And you may have miss the bus.

Wait a minute, let me take you home.

Sorry, but it is my fault. Let me run back grab my things. In the mean while just meet me at the back step.

Okay thanks, Penny went on to clock out.

We don't need other see us together. It may be trouble in our neighed hood.

You already know what they already thinking. This is your first day. They see us talking. Paul yelled.

Oh, and you make a good point.

I walked toward the backside door. Some of the ladies looked at me funny. And roll their eyes me.

Wow, I wondered what I done to them for act like that. To have player hater already they don't know me.

I got to tell Freedom about this one. Penny whispered to herself. Hey, why that funny look on your face? Paul walk up.

Oh, I already got player hate. What you mean?

Oh, some of these ladies just walk by and rolled their eyes at me.

Wow, they must be afraid of you.

Let go home. Paul smile.

Yes, I'm ready. Penny shake her head.

Let me call Freedom see what she up too?

The phone just ring and ring. I wondered why she isn't answer her phone. Let me text maybe see it.

Hey, who is calling? If I may ask Paul opened the door for her. Oh, my friend but she isn't answering her phone.

She probably still trying to run behind this man she met. What you mean? She running behind a man?

That what I said Penny look up.

She isn't suppose to running behind no man. Do she know what the bible on that subject?

Yes, I been preaching this to her for the longer. So far she isn't trying hear that.

She told me she looking for a rich man take her. Paul burst out laugh.

That book of Proverb.

Whoso findeth a wife a good thing, and obtaineth favour of the Lord.

Sorry, now days these men isn't trying take a woman. Unless she do the same.

Yeah, I know that right. But I'm isn't look.

Finally, the phone ring it was Freedom.

Paul, excuse me for a second. This is my friend. Okay, I be waiting in the car.

Girl, why you haven't answer your phone. Sorry, but I have a life too.

Oh, excuse me I just trying to check on you.

Miss. Smart mouth.

I'm okay. I just got off the phone with my future husband. What? Freedom stop lying.

Girl, please I don't have too.

Well, you can cancel our girl outer tonight.

Hey, are sure about that? I buy some food for us. Sorry, just keep it fresh. I see you tomorrow night. I got a date with my man.

Did I ask you stop lying? What number you have?

Girl, I will tell you later about that. I got to go. So I can get myself ready.

I don't want keep my man waiting.

Okay, you better call tonight. Let me know you okay.

Wow why that surprise look on your face. Paul smile. Oh, Freedom say she have a date.

Okay!

Well, that mean I'm be having dinner along tonight In that case let me take you out for dinner.

What you asking me out? Paul look over at her. Yeah, if you accept.

It sound good but I already owe you. I think I will stick around the house. Maybe read couple page one of the book. Plus I'm going wait on Freedom called.

Okay, I understand maybe another time.

Yeah, sorry but I do appreciate the ride. As Penny getting her things out the car.

Miss. Penny I will see you in the morning. Paul smile. Okay, I'll be there.

Well, let me jump in the shower. And find some to wear for tonight. Freedom running around trying to get it together.

Let me call Peter see if he didn't change his mind for tonight.

Penny going to talk about me so bad. If she find out what I'm up too.

So I will keep this to myself.

Hey, Mr. Britt I hope you isn't busy.

Okay, give me a few minute get some of this black nasty coffee. I'll be all ear.

Thanks!

Yes! Mr. Britt grab the newspaper sat down.

Do you remember me telling about a woman I met?

Yeah, you gave her your number. But I didn't understand that. She call me asking me do I want to hang out tonight.

Oh, really! What you going to do?

Mr. Britt you know I said yes. Plus I wont have to sitting around the house alone.

But I hope she isn't trying to go to a high end restaurant. Because I just pay my rent. I don't have the money. Peter shaking his head.

Boy, you so crazy. How you trying be a playboy?

If you broke. You know these women don't want to go Mc Donald. They can take their self.

I think you better take out a loan. Or find something to pawn. Mr. Britt burst out laughing.

Man, I'm isn't trying to do all that just be with a woman. I hope she isn't like that. Plus I hope she have her own money.

Oh, I forget ask him what time he going to pick me up. I better call before I get ready. Freedom whispered to herself.

Peter getting ready go to the restroom before the bell rang. His phone ring.

I wondered who called me. I grab my phone look at it. It was Freedom.

I hope her calling me to cancel the plan for the night. Because I don't have any play money right now.

Hello, this is Freedom. Yes, what up?

Oh, I forget ask you what time should I be ready.

Aw, aw I don't know. Peter shake his head. Thinking what he got his self into.

Well, I be ready about 7:30. I text you my address. So you won't have any excused not to pick me up.

Okay!

You have wonderful day at work. Freedom smile. Oh, thanks.

Wait a minute did I just got play?

Yeah! She got me. That my job be the player. Now I got to step up my game.

Well, Mr. Britt maybe right I do need a small loan.

I better called my friend to see if he can hook me up. And ask him could I borrow some money.

And one of his outfit for tonight. I won't let her play me again. I'm the man with a good plan.

Peter thought to his self as he walking out the restroom.

Little each other don't know they're trying to play each other's.

Well, I better stop by mom house before we go on our little date. To see if I can borrow some money. if I have to catch the bus back home. Or pay for my own meal he just might go to the restroom. And he never come back. Then I be stuck with the bills.

Na, he won't do that. But if he do I will hunt him down. And I will mess up his little world. Freedom thinking to herself. As she getting ready for date.

Wow, I better run up out here soon the bell rang. I can't be late.

I don't want give her something to talk about.

I can't be trusted and I'm a liar. So I better get something together. And show her a nice time.

Even though so ask me out. And she sound like a pushed woman.

Now what I'm going to wear. I don't want over dress or under dress. I want this night my remembering. And this is our first date.

Hey, Peter where you going on your date tonight? Mr. Britt yell up to him.

Well, I don't know. Because I wasn't the one who ask.

I hope she got somewhere she wanted to go. And have the some money.

How could you be a playboy when you broke? Man, you need a part time job.

Oh, no I can't handle that.

What you mean?

I know you heard that old saying. What? Peter yell down to him.

If a man don't work. He don't eat. Mr. Britt smile. But I won't have time to wine and dine the ladies.

Man, you just foolish. Mr. Britt throw his hands in the air. While he walk around to the restroom.

Mr. Britt may have a good idea. Na, I don't think so. I be alright.

The ball rang.

I better get my things together. Before I be the last one in line.

Hey, Mr. Britt I see you in the morning. Okay, I rushing to the clock.

Boy, I got to get out here before I get caught up in this traffic. Then I know I will be later Peter walking out the door.

Hey, what wrong with you? Talking I'm to yourself. Are you gone crazy. Another co- worker yelled.

Na, man I have date tonight. And I can't be late. Because this woman may be my wife.

Oh, sorry in that case let me get out of your way. Thanks Peter smile.

Hey, Guys please let this man though.

Why? We all have long day and ready go home too.

This man have a hot date. Let us pray this may be his wife soon. Okay, if that so he owe us invite to bachelor party.

Yes, I think we have a deal. Peter yell as running though the line. Thanks Guys, maybe we can hang out after work sometimes.

Okay, the guys yell back.

Oh, boy I better hurry I put something to wear. I don't have long before my man arise.

Plus I got do something with my wig.

I don't want sacred him away on our first date. The phone rang.

Now, who calling me? I don't have time talk to them. I know only Satan trying to stop me getting my man.

Let me grab this phone tell them I will call them back later. It was Penny.

Girl, what you want? I trying get ready for my date.

Do you need me go with you? Keep my eyes on you. Na, Girl I can handle it.

But thanks anyway. Freedom putting on her makeup.

Sorry Penny, I got to go now. I'm trying put my face together. Okay, you better some pictures. I want to see this man. You been chase down for months.

Okay, I will bye Girl.

I will call you later together.

Okay, Penny looking in the refrigerator.

Lord, please watch over my girl. She isn't thinking what she doing.

I hope no one else want to talk. I throw my clothes on now. As she trying to find her shoes.

By that time the phone rang again.

Now I can't be up here trying to talking. I got to get out of here before I'll late.

I wondering who calling me now. It was dad.

Hey, how are you? I'm okay!

Why you calling? Freedom shaking her head.

What? I thought I was your father.

So why you asking me so many question?

Is this a crime a dad want to talk to his daughter?

I haven't see you in two week. And someone don't know how to pick up a phone check on their parents

Aw, sorry Dad! I been busy.

Oh, you don't have time for me. You must got a man now. He taking all your times.

No, dad I'm isn't saying that.

So what are you saying my daughter?

Nothing dad! What on your mind?

I'm just bored. Your mother gone with her Holy friends. Thanks you Jesus!

Sorry, dad I got to go. I promise I will call you tomorrow. That okay, your mother will be there to worry me death. Aw, Dad! I hope mom still got that bury insurance on you. Now, you have jokes.

Na, dad because if you don't have some. I guess we got to burn you. Because it cheap and quick.

Girl, I'm going remember that.

When you ask for another plate. Oh, dad!

What now? I thought you have something to do.

Yes! I do. I need you drop by my house pick up these dishes. I know mom miss them.

Na, that isnt going to happen.

You take out here and you going bring them.

I know, I better leave you alone before something bad happen to you.

Bye!

Wow, why this night trying work against me?

I been working hard to make this night happen. Now I don't know what to think.

A thought came to her if a man fined a wife is a good thing.

Aw, I forget that I'm going to get this man. I'm tired of being alone. I want someone take care of me for a change. So I can sit back relax enjoy life. Instead of me have to hit the clock every morning. When I get paid. I got to pay it all out on bills.

And sometimes I barely have enough money make it. Until I get paid again. I'm sick of tired of it. I want some help and I will make myself love him. As she was thinking while finished up dressing.

Now I'm ready this man better be not late. Freedom waiting on Pete called.

Chapter 17

This can't Be Happened To me

Peter jump into the car spin out the parking lot. Hoping he can get home soon. But he forget to call his friend Jack. To ask for a loan.

He was halfway home. Before he realize he didn't call Jack.

Aw, man I better pull over and call him. I hope he answered his phone. Lately he been out of town.

Lord, please let this man answered his phone. I need this loan. I don't want go without some money in my pocket. It look bad if she ask for something to eat.

So I won't have to if I skip out on her. I pray everything be his favor.

Hey, man I'm glad you answer your phone. Man, you so hard to keep up with.

Well, yea my job keep on the go. My girl thinking I'm cheating on her because of it.

But she must forgot I get to pay the bills. Or we both be homeless. Then again she can get a better paying job. So I can stay at home. I be the maiden.

Wow, so you going to put on the dress too. Peter burst out laughing.

Na, that isn't going to happen. Now, you can stop tripping.

Hey, what going with you? I know you didn't stop by here for nothing. You always take something back with you.

Well, I can't help myself.

Oh, I just need a favor. Peter smiling. Okay!

What you need?

Well, I need to borrow a hundred dollar. Until a better day. I have a hot date tonight. Maybe she will be my baby mother.

Oh, really in that case hurry up come get it. You been lonely long time.

Aw, man thanks you just made my day.

But you say that about every woman you meet. Jack burst laughing.

Well, yea I got to think positive my brother. It going to happen someday. You know pimping isn't easy anymore. If you don't be careful these women out here be pimping you out.

What you mean? Jack sat down.

Just like your old lady got you out here make the money. She already know you going to bring home the bacon.(money). If you don't she going to lock it up.

And she have the master key too.

Boy, I know you was little crazy. At first I didn't want believe it. Now I need buy you a strait jacket. Before you hurt yourself.

Because you lost your mind.

Oh, I also need to jump in your closet. Borrow one of your outfit too.

Man, do I need to go on the date for you too? Jack smile. Na, remembered you got a woman. And I don't think she wouldn't like it. Maybe we could go out on a double date sometimes.

First I got to make sure she the one.

Man, you so foolish.

Yeah, I don't want to be wasting my time on her. When I could be looking for someone else.

Man, you need some patient. Let see what happen first before you judge her.

Okay, okay, you're right Pete shaking his head.

Bye! You better call me later. I want to know what happen. Jack smiling.

Okay, you just want to be noise.

Well, yeah! Why not? Peter you done it to me.

Peter can't couldn't say nothing. Knowing he was right.

I think Peter isn't going to show up. Freedom looking up at the clock. She starting thinking what Penny been preaching to her stop running behind this man. If he want you he will show you.

Tears in her eyes whisper why I been a fool. Thinking he was going to love me.

And he going to take care for me. So she started changing her clothes.

By this time the phone rang. This got be Peter calling.

Freedom started getting happy. She slowly looking down at the phone. It was Penny.

I can't answered this call. Because she going to asking too many question.

Why this? Why that? I'm isn't ready answered her questions. I throw the phone on the bed.

Aw, man I'm running late. This traffic started getting back up. I better call Freedom let her know I'm stuck in traffic. But I'm on my way.

Oh wow, my phone is dead. Now she going to think I'm lying to her. What I'm going to do now?

Hey, I wondered what going on with Freedom. I started to worry because she isn't picking up her phone.

Should I throw some clothes jump on the bus? To see if my friend okay. Lord

Na, I better not maybe she is having fun. And she don't want to be disturb.

Oh, well I better jump into the shower. And get ready for bed. Maybe I grab one of the book Paul gave me to study.

Tears just roll down Freedom eyes. Wishing Peter would call let her know if he cancel the date.

Yeah, Penny is right. It was a bad idea chasing a man. When he don't want to be caught.

I give up on men. They just all liar. And they want what between a woman legs. I refuse go down that road with any man. Just for someone to take care of me.

Let me call Penny apologize to her.

Because she was right. All this time I been running behind this man. And look what happen. Ask she getting ready take off her make up.

Hey, I better find a phone quick. To let Freedom her know I'm running late. I hope some battery life in my phone find her number. He pull into a busy parking lot. Hope someone allow him use their phone.

Please, Mr. could I borrow your phone. I got call my friend. We suppose go on a date. And I'm running late because of this traffic. I know she think I'm isn't going to keep my words.

Okay, thanks.

It just ring and ring.

No, answered, Lord I mess up.

Now, how I know if she going to be the one.

That sound like my phone ringing. Let me grab it hope it Peter. I run out the bathroom. But it was too late.

Let me call back. Maybe he will answer it. Hello, Peter are we still going on our date?

Ma, sorry my name isn't Peter. But if you want to go on a date. Give me your air dress I be there in hour.

No, thank.

Okay, but keep my number in case. If Peter don't show up. I hang up the phone.

Wow, I had tears in my eyes. Wondering why he haven't call.

Oh, man that must been Peter who used my phone. And that the lady he suppose have a date with.

Let me try her call back. And tell her it Peter trying contract you. Because he running late.

I hope she answer my call. Or Peter going to be in big trouble.

Freedom, just stood there wondering why this man call me out of the blue. Asking me go on a date with him.

Why everything isn't going my way tonight?

By that time her phone was ring again.

I wondering who this playing game with me.

Waiting a minute it is the same number I just call early. Yes!

Hello, may I help you?

Well, no I want to help you. Please don't hang up.

First, of all I'm sorry for been rude to you early. But a young man use my phone. He was telling me he was running for a date. He said his phone was dead. And I let him use my phone.

Oh yeah! Freedom getting happy. Because she put it together. Thanks for let me know.

Oh, you're welcome. I hope you have good night.

Oh, wow let me get myself back together. Before Peter pull up.

I hope Freedom having fun. Penny thought to herself. As she getting ready grab a book.

By that time the phone.

This must Freedom going to tell how her night going. I grab the phone.

Hello, girl what up? How your night going?

Well, my night going fine. And I hope your going great also. Hey, wait a minute you isn't my friend Freedom.

No, this Paul.

What? Why you calling me this time of the night. Sorry, I hope I didn't disturb you. I couldn't sleep.

No, but I'm surprise you calling after hour.

Sorry again, I thought I give you a called. To see if you need me help you study.

Wow, I just about to grab one of the book. Well, since you call and you are my boss.

I can't turn down your help. Because I need my j o b. Your sister got bills.

Paul, bust out laughing.

Hey, what so funny? You?

I'm telling the truth. And let be clear I'm not looking for someone take care of me. I been there and done that. It didn't work out well. I end up taking care a man. So we going to be adult right.

What you mean?

Other word we both going keep our eyes and hands to ourselves.

Now concerning the things of which you wrote to me:

It is good for a man touch a woman. Nevertheless, because sexual immorality, let each man his own wife, and let each woman have her own husband.

Okay, I promise. I been be good.

Hold on, I didn't call you to hit on you. Be honest I can't sleep. I thought I call to see if you needed the help. I know some of the books can confused.

Oh, sorry!

It okay, I probably feel the same way my boss called. Paul, smile.

Well, since call you me how long you been at the Law firm?

My parents work there and in the summer time. I help them around the office. Running erred, clean up while they working.

So, when I finished school. I went to collage become a lawyer. I been there 15 years.

What? Now that a long time. Yeah!

He didn't want her know I'm is the owner. Because his parents die left him everything. And they told his take care of his little sister.

I don't know I can do that? Penny burst out laughing.

Well, I didn't thought I been there this long myself. I guess time creep up on me. Don't get me wrong I been though some rough time. I had to hold my head up. Still maintain especially when my mother died. So other wouldn't feel sorry for me.

Then not long my father went into depression because my mother death. And he pass away too. I had deal with my sister craziness because she is the baby.

My parents spoiled her. And she went out of control. On top of that she had kids. The baby daddy isn't around. I had to step up be a father figure to them. They was heading to the foster care. And I couldn't let that happen. But if I didn't have God on my side. I probably too lost my mind.

Wow! You sound like a good man.

Yeah, that my life. Everyone don't know my past. So please, keep it quit.

The women on the job don't need to know.

Oh, don't worry. I promise.

Penny, started feeling funny. Why this man telling about his self.

And he didn't ask me open the book. So he can help me study.

Well, my friend it getting late. I better let you get some sleep now. Work in the morning.

Yeah, I know that right.

Well, be ready around 7am. I will pick up.

Oh, you don't have too. I can caught the bus. I don't want you go out of your way for me.

Yes, I know but I want to do it. Isn't no problem. Just keep it to yourself. I'm isn't trying be a taxi for the Law firm.

Now, you're silly.

Yeah, I for real.

Because I have so many women try sleep with me. But isn't going to happen. I been raise better than that. And I can't afford get in trouble with the office.

Wow!

Okay, I won't turn down a free ride. I well save my 2 dollar for my break. You know your sister do get hungry too.

You're so silly. I see you in the morning.

And you have a good night.

Why this man been so nice to me. I know I'm not a beauty queen. Or Miss. American. I hope he don't think I'm give up these panties. Now that isn't going happy. Until someone put a rock on my finger. I play alone with him.

Now concerning the things whereof ye wrote unto me. It is good for a man not to tough a woman.

Nevertheless, let every man have his own wife, and let every woman have her own husband.

Just to see what he really up too. Penny roll over turn off the light.

Aw, man I hope Freedom don't think I cancel the date. Peter rushing down the road.

I finally made to Freedom house. Boy I hope I'm not too late. Plus I hope this is the right address. This night been really mess up. What I had to though go to get here. Let me knock this door. I can't call her because my phone is dead. Peter whisper as he getting out of the car. Maybe I need to leave my car door opened. In case I knock on the wrong house. And I have to run.

Chapter 18

The heat Is On

Wow, you really show up. Freedom grab her coat.

Yes, I'm sorry for running late. It was accident on the road. And I had wait until the road was clear. Also I was rushing to get ready. And I forget put my on the changer. While I was getting dress. Now it dead. Pete stood in the door.

Okay, let go!

Oh, let me open your door for you. Thanks!

Wow, that what a man supposedly do. Be a gentleman. Freedom smiling as getting in the car.

Where you wanted to go to eat? Peter turn on some slow music.

I know don't. It been a long time since I went on a real date. Oh, really! Somebody beauty like you shouldn't have no problem.

Yes, I know but I been running into loser lately. They isn't on my lever.

And I don't have time to teach them. What you mean?

See, a lot of them looking for their mother. In a woman someone to take care of them. And I isn't going to do that anymore. I got caught up one or twice in my younger days. Thinking if I don't this or that for him will leave me. I almost lost my apartment fooling with one guy. I was trying to buy his affection. I find out he was looking at the girl next door. Here I'm trying keep the bills pay. While he was wine and dine her off of my money.

When I found out what he doing. Playing with my money. I whip him like a kids for taking my money giving to someone else.

Peter got quiet.

You okay? You don't have much to say. Aw, I'm just listing to you.

But I ran into some women looking for their daddy. Please explain! Freedom look over at him.

Okay, other word some these women looking for a man take care of them and their kids. Because the kids father isn't in the life. So they figure a piece of man better then nothing.

What? Peter look upside her head. Thinking this woman she be must crazy. And think I'm would get into a relationship like that. No that isn't me.

Oh, what wrong with that. I think that his job.

Aw, sorry I really don't agree with all that a package deal. The kids include. Peter smile

Why? We all have our own opinion.

That true.

Here the thing I believe in a woman should help out that man. If in a relationship or married. That what I was told by father. Peter turn down the music.

Well, it sound like your father a demand man. He wanted everything his way.

No, he wasn't like that. He work and pay bills. But mom she also work to make up the difference to keep the household run smooth.

Wow! Freedom couldn't believe what she was hearing. Yep!

Well, that isn't going to happen to me. I'm going take a break from work. I know he got a lot of money. I know he isn't thinking I'm going to work when he put this ring on my finger. He trying play hard to catch and he cheap too.

Maybe he don't want me to know have bank (money).

So ought men to love their wives as their own bodies. He that loveth his wife loveth himself.

I just play alone with him little game. I'm fine with that. Freedom whispered under her breathe.

Yes, she trying play me thinking if I get with her. I'm going to take care her. While she laying around the doing nothing. Oh no, I'm not going fall for that trap. Mom help dad out. If she the one. She still going to work. Hit that old clock too. Dad told me, And the Lord God said, it is not good that the man should be alone; I will make him an help meet for him.

Two are better than one; because they have a good reward for their labour I'm will play alone with her. And what she really up too. Peter whisper to himself.

Okay! Where we going?

You have any suggesting? My beautiful Queen.

Wait what you said? Freedom have surprise look on her face. Beautiful Queen. Peter smile.

Oh! Thanks. Freedom whisper under her breathe. I must doing something right.

No!

I know where we can go it nice bar q place.

Oh, yep! I hadn't bar q in a long time. Okay that sound good. Freedom smile.

It name Bo's bar-q on 13 and Bullet Ave.

I can't wait tell Penny where we went on our date.

I hope he don't skip out on me. And leave me with the bills. Freedom whisper under her breathe.

Yes, I can handle this.

I won't order nothing under 30 dollar. I just let her order whatever. Peter smile.

Mr. Paul I have special sitting for you. I think you and guess would like it.

Okay, Peter look at waitress stranger.

Hold on I'm not Paul but I accept it. This waitress got me mix up with someone else. Maybe I can get some discount off the food.

Hey, see you have a different woman tonight. If I was you like loaded (money) I think I would do the same. Just see how long can I play. The waitress whisper. Peter just smile.

May, I got you something to drink. While you look over the menu.

Yes! Please.

Ma, what would like drink?

Oh give me the finest wine you have to drink. Pete almost get chore.

Are you okay sir?

Yes, may I have a glass water to clear my throat? Yes, sir I will back shortly.

Thank you! Peter smile

I see everything look so good to eat.

Freedom can't believe she is in a beautiful restaurant this. Yes, I know.

I hoping she don't want the higher thing on the menu. Because I don't want be embarrass. If can't pay for the dinner.

Little Freedom know Penny had her interview here with Paul. That why the waitress didn't know Paul and Peter was twins.

And Peter think it was stranger that the waitress get him mix up someone else.

Hey, I didn't heard correctly the waitress call you Paul.

Yes, maybe I have a twin out here something. Or have someone look like me. Peter smile.

I better roll out of this bed. I don't want Paul be waiting on me. Because he already going out his way pick me.

So, I won't take advance of him. Penny ran to the restroom jump the shower.

I better start dress down because I don't want Penny know who I'm really is. She might look at me difference.

I just want her look at me just another co- worker. I hope nobody tell her before I do. I am the boss.

Good morning, Boss.

Hey, come in my officer please.

Rich, please don't call me boss. I don't want everyone know who I'm.

Okay! Why? Are you okay? Did someone threatening you. Oh you trying hide out from someone?

No, I'm fine. I just need you trade place with me. Boss I don't understand. What you really up too? Nothing! Paul looking around.

Oh, you are sure you want to do my job?

Yes, I know can handle it. Paul removed his name off his desk.

Okay, now I can give myself a bonus and a little rise. I been ask for years. Since, I don't need your approved now. Oh, are you giving the right to fired people also.

Na, because I know you fired everyone up in here. These women would whip you all over this place. Your wife won't know who you are. Because all those knots be on your face. She going to think you trying rob her. And she grab your Louisville slugger bat. And work you some more. I need you alive. So I'm going to you a favor. No! You can not. Paul shaking his head.

No, fair! You won't be no power. And you want become you. Rich sit down at the desk. This how is feel being a boss. Huh

Yes, I guess. It just a job to me. Maybe one day I retired let you run in my place.

Yes, right that isn't going to happen. Paul you need stop tripping. Hey, it cross my mind couple time.

Maybe when I find the one. We just might travel around the world. I haven't been out the county yet. Because I didn't want go alone.

Oh, you forget me! My suitcase always pack. Rich look at him. Man, shut up you have a family. And I'm trying get them mad at me. You know I'm isn't in shape. I can't be running might have heart attack. And I'm ready to leave here yet.

Oh, you not friend no more. You hope I die off before you my time. You better pray you don't beat me out.

Bye, Rick I got pick up our new employee.

Hey, you need started wearing suits to work a couple weeks. While I'm figure out your job.

Okay, why you out I think you need hook me you with some suits. Because my maybe little old fashion.

Oh, I knew it was going to cost me. Boy, I just can't win around you.

No, I can't give myself rise. Or I can't go around the world with you. Did you forget life isn't free?

Now, you telling on yourself. Huh

Rick, I really got to go. I don't want be late.

Oh, now you run out on me. Because I'm figure out what you trying to do.

Well, since you know. Now I won't how explain it to you. Paul walk toward the door.

Good morning, Miss. Gail!

Good morning you too Paul.

Why you rushing of the door? Gail smile as she putting some paper away.

Ask Rich he will fill you in. Paul throw is hand the air.

Hey, Rich why Boss run out the door. Girl, you can't call him boss anymore.

What? Why?

Because I'm your new boss now. No, brother you can't be my boss.

Why? Too bad Rich standing in the door smiling.

You already know you and me always auger too much around here. And I win all the fight.

Na, that not truth. I just get tried hearing your mouth sometimes. So I give up and leave you alone.

But I promise I'm going to be good. If you promise that you whole your tongue before you speak.

Death and life are in the power of the tongue: and they that love it shall eat the fruit thereof.

Now, you really trying get on my nerve today.

I bought us some lunch see how you acting up.

But you still haven't told why you say you the boss now. All suddenly.

Okay, you can't tell no one.

Okay, okay, tell me I don't have all day. I got thing to do. Rich. See, Gail your mouth just might get you trouble. So shut it.

Rich just spill your gut like you always doesn't.

Okay, I and Paul trade job for couple weeks. Because he don't want someone know he the boss.

Oh, I knew that already. Because he can't keep his eyes off the new hire. Miss Penny.

Oh yep I saw that too. This maybe the one.

Yep! So we going stay out of their way. Let him do his own things.

So this maybe our time learned how to run this place without him. Someday it may come true. We be already for the task.

So the last be first, and the first last: for many be called, but few chosen.

Yes, Rich you just might a good idea. I know he been talking get marriage someday. And having a family someday.

Wow, Rich I didn't think you had a brain to think like that. Shut-up go back to work.

Boy, I should've left out little early. Now I'm about hit this traffic. I hope no accident on the freeway. Let me call Penny let know I'm on my way.

By that time Freedom was walking to the bus.

Let me call Penny before I get on this noisy bus. Her phone ring and ring.

I know it Freedom calling me. She wanted to tell me about her date last night. But I better finished getting dress. I call her back later.

I also got some juicy news to tell her. About my new manger how her treating like I'm special.

Na, I better keep that part to myself. Let me wake up this man isn't interest in me. I don't have much. I got more bills then money, no car. On top of that my parent gave me this house. Because they wanted some private. Penny started crying thinking she isn't good enough have someone to love her. She just a simple girl.

Little Penny know Paul is very interest to get know her better. By that time Paul drove by the bus stop.

Hey, I know that of my man see me out here trying catch the bus. No knowing I don't have a car. It would be nice he pick me up take me to breakfast. And take me to work. I love see those wanted be women faces when we drive up. They thinking I don't have a man. Someday they going to in shock when I show them the rock on my hand.

When my man ask me to jump the broom.

Ma, Ma, are you riding with us today? The bus driver smile. Oh, oh, yes! Sorry I just having a moment. Freedom smile.

I wish I should've ate breakfast. Now my mind playing trick on this morning.

Maybe I need to slow down this woman isn't going gave me chance. I think she are beautiful and funny. And maybe all the women I try to date. They're right I'm boring. I guess I don't have a life. Because I work too much. Or they thought I was going to throw money at their feet. But that isn't happen. Because they will love the money more than me. I just want a simple woman love me. Lord, I hope nothing wrong that. Paul sitting at the red light.

Look over at the passenger seat wish someone there. Now I will call Freedom back. I hope isn't mad me.

Hello, Miss. Penny. I see you don't have time for me anymore.

Na, that isn't true. You see!

Hold on a minute my ride calling me. Let me put you on hold.

See, I told you she don't have time for me since she got this new job. I thought you was my best friend. I guess not maybe you found some news friend. To hang out tears roll down her.

Hey, Freedom I'm back it was Paul my new co- worker who giving me a ride to work. Wait a minute are you still there.

Aw, man I must hang up on her by accident

I can't call her back right now because my ride round the corner. Let me grab my things. And I hope I didn't forget anything.

Oh, wow I better get out this bed before I run later again. I can't afford do that to many time. I'm be looking for a job. Peter hit the snooze button.

Good morning, Freedom what wrong with your makeup? Miss. Low whisper.

Oh, sorry!

Why you tell me sorry? When you haven't did anything too me.

Well, I got a lot on my mind. Let me go into to this restroom get my face back to   gether. Before the others girls see me. Then I be laugh of the day. I meet you in the break room soon as I finished.

Wow, I can't believe my childhood friend. She isn't my friend anymore?

Maybe she jealous because I got man now. Or she feel the same way. Let me get out this restroom. So I can clock in. And grab me some of this nasty coffee. Tell Miss. Low about my night.

Freedom look back in the mirror.

Chapter 19

Under Cover

Good morning, Miss. Penny.

I hope I wasn't too late. I got catch up in traffic. Paul opened the door for her.

Na, just long I get there. I got to show my boss he can count on me. Whatever my little hands can do. I will make it happen.

Wow, you so excited to go work.

Well, yea! Penny smile as she getting into the car. Not me!

Why?

Well, I been working since I was a young boy. Now I'm all grown up. Isn't fun anymore? Back in the day I was trying impress the women. If you didn't have a car or job. No play with them. Ask my parents can have car for my sixteen birthday.

Did you get the car? Penny smile

Na, but they gave a job and tell I can buy my own. Because they thought I wouldn't appreciate it. If I work for it would teach me how appreciate things. And at that time I didn't know why they treated me with tough love.

It kept me out trouble because didn't have time hang out with my friends. They use to laugh at me while they hanging out. And I was mad at my parents got me working at the law firm with them. I had clean up the offices and those nasty restrooms.

When I got home I still had to do my homework. Then get my clothes together for school. So I won't be late.

Wow! I understand you have good reasoning feeling the way you do. I know what your problem.

Oh yea! What?

You didn't have a life.

You may not realize you allowed your job be your life. What you mean? I don't understand.

Okay, if I'm right let me know. Penny look over at him. I will!

First of all you don't have your own family. Yes I do my sister and nephew and niece.

Yes, I know! But I'm talking about you have a wife or no kids come home too. Sometimes you rather be at work. Instead come home to an empty house. And you see your friends got wife and kids. Yes, you prayed to have the same. Lately you been questioning God. When it going to be my time? I'm a good person. And I don't mind helping others. I go to church and do believe in you.

Paul have tears running his face. Knowing she was right. Why you crying? They told me men don't cry.

But men have emotion too. I love see a man cry. Penny gave him a nap to wash his tears always.

I'm sorry! You didn't supposed to see me do that. But I admit you are right. More I put myself out there. I get my heart broken. Over and over again I give up.

It isn't worth it.

Wait minute isn't over yet. Penny smile.

What you mean? Paul wipe his eyes please keep this to yourself. You can trust me.

Let this be our little secret.

Okay! Penny smile. I can't mess up my good things up.

Paul burst out laughing. Thanks I need that.

Well, maybe you need to leave it alone? And just live yourself life. When it time you will know it. You must learn how guard your heat. If God said it. Believe me it going to happen. But remember he don't work your time. He don't need no help. So please do yourself a favor.

Okay!

Stay out of God way because you holding up your own progress.

Trust in the Lord, and do good; so shalt thou dwell in the land, and verily thou shalt be fed.

Delight thyself also in the Lord: and he shall give thee the desires of thine heart.

Commit the way unto the Lord; trust also in him; and he shall bring it to pass.

Wow, how did you know? Are you a prophets? Did God told you about me?

No, I just look in the mirror and saw my life flash before me. Wow, we have something in comment.

Yep! What? Paul

We are lonely. Well, that true.

The both said at that same time. Not for long.

Paul grab Penny hands.

But neither didn't know God was putting things in place for the both.

And we know that all things work together for good to them that love God, to them who are the called according to his purpose.

Before they knew it they in the parking lot.

Hey, Penny I'm going in though the side door. I don't need too many eyes on me. I will be talk of the day.

Okay!

I need you come in the front door.

Aw, man I hope my knees don't give out. Because I didn't have my breakfast this morning.

I get to find away take a picture my man. Maybe the ladies will close their mouth. I know I haven't lost mind. And I'm not crazy. Oh, I know what I can do. I will invite Peter to church. I walk up and stand by him. And get someone take our picture together.

Then I some evidence show them. Maybe Penny would come with me. Na, that isn't going to happen.

So I better leave that one long.

I will call him on my lunch break. Freedom smiling to herself.

Lord, look over there that girl really lost it. Ever since she told us she got a man.

That make me wondered if she making up this things about this man.

Miss. Low maybe we need to keep an eye on her. If started talking to herself and smiling. We need to hurry up tell the boss. I he can call the mental hospital to bring her a strait jacket. We don't need her hurt herself or no one else either. Miss. Conner whisper.

Yes, I know I don't want to be any witness. Showing my face on the news. They might find out I have a lot parking tickets I haven't pay yet. Then they be laughing at me going out the door to jail.

Mrs. Joan! What?

Good morning, Miss. Penny. I see you with a smile on your face. Yep, I'm ready get this day started. Penny smile.

Great, I'm glad you feel good. Because you may have a long day. We have some new clients be here in an hour. So I need you hurry up bring your things put in here. And run around the corner store get some donuts and coffee.

Okay, I will do.

Thanks, while I'm getting our profile together. So we won't have no problem get started. Here our business card that we use buys things with.

Okay, I'm ready! Let me put back on my coat.

Thanks again Gail smile.

Penny put the card in her pocket. Walking out the door. Ma, ma did you drop this card?

I don't know! Let check. Aw think I did. Thanks Mr. you have a bless day.

You too ma.

Let look at this card make sure I didn't take someone else card. Paul Donald.

Oh, I think Gail gave me the wrong card. Let me call back to the office.

Hello, this is Gail at Donald's Law firm. Yes, this is Penny.

Is something wrong?

That the problem I don't know.

You gave this card it have Paul name on it.

Oh, nothing wrong. Our boss had it made for Paul. When he go out to a business meeting. So it okay to use it

Oh okay! Thanks I'm didn't want get into trouble for using it. Girl, you fine!

By that time Paul walk in the office.

Hey, you owe me one? Gail look up. How?

Penny, saw your name on a credit card. I gave her to use to buy some things before our new customer coming in today.

I sent her buy some donuts and coffee.

Oh, did you took care it for me. Yes, I lie for you.

Oh, I'm sorry. I will send you and your husband on a date. Whatever you want to eat. And I take care the bills

Wow, I take that it. Before you change your mind. Gail smile.

I just don't want know right now. Maybe she is the one for me. I knew it.

How you know? Did Rich told you?

No, I'm woman too. I know when a man flirting. And how you look at her. Plus how you go out of your way doing things for her.

Aw, I just can't hide nothing for you.

No! But you have my blessing. I will let you handle your business. But you must keep in form me of everything. Maybe I can help hook up my brother.

So we can go ahead talk about this bonus you going to give me. So next year for my vacation I can go on this cruise. I been dreaming for years.

Okay, okay, you win. Boy, you and Rich always trying trip me up. Na, we just be looking for you. Boss Gail whispered.

I rest my case.

Yep, I think so too. Burst of laughing. That why I love you my Sister.

By that time Penny walk in the office. Excuse I hope didn't interrupt you too.

Na, Gail was telling me how great you doing. Yes, whatever !

Okay, where you want me put those donuts and coffee? Oh, take it in the comfort room.

Okay! Oh here the card back and the receipt. Thanks.

Hey, Paul I think she walk in heard you when you said you love me. Gail whisper.

Oh, no! Now it over trying get with her.

Yep! Sorry my brother. Now there go my bonus. Gail drop her head.

What can I do make things right.

I don't know! But I just might considered giving the bonus. Paul had a upset look on his face.

Gail, I need you help me out of a jam. I owe you one. I want get to know her first.

Maybe nothing become something. Wow, you really like this girl.

Yes, I got make thing right.

Plus I want take my vacation too. Gail start thinking how she going to pull it off.

I knew Paul isn't interest in me. I mighty well stop hoping something good can come of this. Penny too had tear in her eyes. Knowing she really started liking Paul.

Hey, Freedom are ready for lunch. Yes! Why?

The bell about the ring.

Yep, but you go ahead I got something to do first. I catch up with you later.

Okay! Miss. Low smile and looking back at Mrs. Conner. I told you something isn't right with her. Now I bet you believe me.

Yep, you're Right! Miss. Low.

We better look for us a place to hide. If she go off up in here. You might have a good point there. I got a family looking for me to come back home. The same way left. Mrs. Conner looking around.

Well, me too. Plus I'm isn't ready meet the creator yet. A lot I things to do.

What?

Repent and confess all my evil way. I want see that man who made me. So I can personal thanks him.

Well, I need to you join too. But not right now. Miss. Low burst out laughing. Girl, too silly.

Let go eat before it be too late.

I hope this man answered this phone. I need get this picture.

So I can have the last laugh. Freedom whispered to herself. As she walking toward the restroom.

Hey, good morning Peter. How was your date? I knew you going to ask me that.

Yep! That me Mr. Britt smile.

Oh, it went well but we have a different opinion on things. What you mean?

She playing broke. But I know she got the money. I think you want a man take of her. I'm isn't feeling that. I think if we get together I'm will work with her to make something happen.

Also thanks God I had enough money take care of our dinner. Boy, you funny.

No, I didn't have to wash any dishes nor skip out on her. I tried that before in my younger days.

But they catch me at the side door. And they made me wash the dishes at least 3 hour.

Okay, I'm glad you didn't either. Because she probably whip your behind. These women now day don't mess up your world up. So you better handle them with care.

It better to dwell in the wilderness, than with a contentious and an angry woman.

Ask Larry one of our co- worker. His wife hit him up side his head with a metal flesh light. Because he came home late being out with the boy all night. He wanted to start a fight. But she got the first lick in. And he wore a knot for two week.

He was going around telling the boys the dog knock him down. And he hit the coffee table. He didn't know his wife was friend of Joe wife. Another co-worker he work here too. And the wife spill her guts. All the boys joke him for days.

Wow! Now that mess up. Peter shaking his head.

The phone rang.

I wondered who calling me? It Freedom!

Excuse Mr. Britt.

Okay, I'm going to warm up my food.

Hello!

Hey, Peter how are you doing?

I'm okay! I'm just getting ready to eat lunch. Okay, I'm sorry for disturb you.

It okay! So what on your mind?

Oh, I wondering would you like go to bible study with me tomorrow night.

Oh, I don't about that. I have something to do. Okay I understand. Sorry for bought you.

No, it okay maybe next time. I be glad to go with you

You have a good day. I got go eat before the bell rang. Freedom I call you when I get off work.

Okay, I talk to you later.

Wow, he just mess up my hold day. Now I can't get that picture I need. Well, let me go hear these ladies mouth. I know they going to think I'm losing it. So I better keep my mouth close. And let them do all the talking. I hope the bell ring soon. Maybe they won't ask me so many questions about my man.

Freedom whisper under her breathe while walking from the restroom.

Chapter 20

Awake Up Call

Hey, Miss. Penny! Yes!
I need you help me in the comfort room for the rest of the day.
Okay! Penny smile.

No, no, Gail come in this office. Excuse, us for one minute.

I wondered what is all about it. Penny stood at the door. What? Now Paul.

Why you invite Penny to help you?

So, I can let her know   how me and you don't have nothing going on. But work.

Okay, that fine too. But you didn't forget? What?

Gail had a funny look on her face.

I'm the real boss. And I got be in this meeting later today. And Penny going to know who I'm. Because Rich still in training. He isn't ready yet.

Gail, drop head my bad. Lord, I better think fast before your clients come in. And mess up your little white lie.

I heard you. Yep! You better very soon. Right now I don't see your vacation in my crystal ball.

What you mean? Paul don't you mess with my vacation. You know I need that.

Okay, I will fix it right now.

Thanks! That my girl. Paul smile and walk out the room. You're so mean but I still love you my brother.

Miss. Penny it a change of plan.

Okay! I'm fine with that. I'm not good around people work up in the big white house.

Well, great! I have a film you need to watch. It going show how to file away paper work.

It will take an hour.

Okay, I better go to the restroom before you started it. Wow, that was close one.

As, Penny walk toward to the restroom. She heard of some of the women whispered.

Saying who she thinking she is this and that more because she close the man.

She turn around they got quiet and walk on down the hall. I wondered what man they're was talking about

Penny thought to herself as she enter the restroom, Let me quickly call Freedom to check on her. The phone rang.

Excuse me lady this maybe my man call me back. Okay!

Let see who really calling me? It Penny!

I wondered why she calling me now. She don't have time for me. I don't know if I should answer this phone.

Wow, she isn't going to answer my call. Okay, she going be alright. Let me get back around the corner. I can't let her childish self-mess up my focus. Before I be out that door. I been praying so long a find a job like this. Tears run down Penny face.

Hey, is that your man? Miss. Conner yelled.

Yes, he wanted me go with him to bible study with tomorrow night. That where we met.

Wow, are your man a Christian?

Well, something like that! Freedom drop her head. Knowing she is lying.

But those things which proceed out the mouth come forth from the heart; and they defile the man.

Because she didn't want them know the truth. She the one chasing behind this man.

Mr. Britt! Yes!

It was Freedom. The girl I went out on a date with last Saturday. Okay! You must did something right.

Well, I thought I treated her like a lady. And I pay for her dinner.

Boy, you so foolish. That what a real man do when take a lady out. Mr. Britt smile.

Na, we should've went half and half on the dinner. Why?

Because she order the most expense food on the menu. That way I could've keep part of the money for gas.

Bye! You don't make any sense. Now I see why you lonely? You too cheap!

No, don't leave yet. She wanted me go to bible study tomorrow night.

Okay, are she a Christian? Or she just playing church. I don't know! That where we met.

But I told her I had something to do. Peter grab a cup of coffee.

Well, I am still going. It doesn't matter he did want go with me. Maybe something will catch my eyes. Or I just need hear the word. Maybe it will change my minds about him. While I'm there. Freedom walking back her machine.

Hey, why you so quiet? Freedom

Sorry, I'm just thinking what I'm going to wear for my man tomorrow.

Okay, I see you later. Oh, what church you belong too? Aw, St. Matthew on the corner 26st maple st.

Okay, Miss. Low.

May I catch you there one Sunday? Oh, really!

Yep!

Oh, just let know I will save you a good seat. Freedom throw hand in the air waving.

Yea, right that why I won't be there. I will be sick. Because she don't know need to what I'm you doing.

Hello, Penny! Hi Mr. Paul.

I'm going out for lunch. Do you need everything? Aw, no I good. Oh here your card back.

Paul, knew Penny started act funny toward him. By tone of her voice.

Okay, are you sure I take care it. I don't mind you use it long as you needed it.

Thanks, but I'll be alright.

In couple the days I get my first check. So you can keep it. Okay, if you need it before you get paid. I leave it with Gail. You have a good day Mr. Paul.

Okay you do the same also.

Thanks, let go in here watch this film. Penny smile

Oh, Lord I really mess up this time up. I got figure this thing out. Before she slip away.

Paul walk toward the restroom. A small still voice said be patient. It shall come to pass.

He shake his head look around to see who was talking to him. But he was the only person in the hall.

Be careful for nothing; but in everything by prayer and supplication with thanksgiving let your requests be made known unto God.

Wow, let me slap myself while I'm trying play hard. Knowing, I need that card.

Now I guess for the rest of this week I'm going to be on a fast. It want hurt me couple pound. But I don't want lose my coke cola body shape.

Yep! I matter well pray too. Maybe things will turn around. And also I'm going to need a ride home too. Now I got bred somebody for two dollar to catch this bus.

Penny had tears running down her face.

What I'm doing? Let me run in this restroom wash my face. I know I'm isn't falling for this man.

Girl, you right! What are you doing? Your blindness' going to make you miss you blessing.

Huh, Penny turn around to see who was talking to her. But no one wasn't there.

I know my mind playing trick on me again. Maybe I need to be dip back in the water again. So I can see again.

Na, I know she going to be hungry later. I better send Rich out to buy her for something. Put it on her desk. But I don't want her know that bought it. Paul reach in her pocket pullout him phone.

Let me pray before I go into this meeting. I can't afford make any mistake. We need this account because it getting close to Christmas. And I always play the secret angel.

I know my people deserve it and they depend on this. Then I can rest. Paul went into an empty room.

Penny, saw Paul coming out of it.

Excuse me! Miss. Gail I know it may not be any of my business. Yes!

What in the room Paul come out of it.

Please, don't you tell him I told you this is his room? That where he go pray when things bought him.

Oh okay! He is a praying man.

Yep! He got me to do the same thing. I come in.

Another thing Paul like my brother I never had. And I try my best look out for him.

He also do the same thing for me and my family. That why I couldn't try hit on him.

We don't have nothing but works relative. We trying keep this company competitive. So we can all have a job.

Penny, drop her head whispered I feel like a fool now. Maybe now I just might had a chance. If I haven't blew it.

Well, I better hurry up think of something fast. Before this man slip away.

I know I do what I can do? I know how I can surprise him by come to the church tomorrow night. Now I must be a fool for this man.

Oh, I'm beginning act like Freedom. I'm going to church. This isn't me. I got to find something to wear. When I go home today.

Little Penny know Freedom going to be there also. And Freedom going get her eyes full. But she going to think Paul is Peter sitting with Penny.

And she going to think Penny trying take her man.

The fight is on Freedom face turn red. As she walk out the door. Later she going to call Peter accused him. Hitting on her friend. But he going to denied it all.

Because he really don't know what she talking about. Freedom!

Miss. Low yell over to her. Ma!

Let go home and now you can stop day dreaming.

Huh!

Get yourself together so we run up out this place. You don't have to yell at me

I heard you the first time. I'm ready. I got to stop by the grocery store. So I can feed these bad kids of mind. They also went on again fast tonight.

But they finally sent the rest of my food stamp. Because somebody down there try mess me up. Miss. Conner smile. Wow! How you get them? They told me I make too much money. But they taking my money every week for taxes. And I can't get nothing back in return. Now that make someone wanted go down there and go off on them. They treat the stamps like their own. Another thing make me mad.

Why?

When I see they give them to people who don't need it. They be smiling walking though the store with two buggy of food. And the ones who really need it.

They can't it or they have to fight for them. Miss. Low putting on her coat.

Yep! I know right. Ladies, you ready. Yep! Miss. Freedom.

The ladies look at each other.

What your plan tonight? Mrs. Freedom.

Oh, not yet Mrs. She smile but I think it going to be soon. Oh, really!

Yes! I want you to be one of my bridge maiden. So save your money.

Okay! We won't miss that day.

Great! I got to go catch this bus.

Okay, you have good night. Freedom walk out the fast.

Thanks same to you.

Why her so called boyfriend won't pick up from work. Because I want to see this man for myself. Miss. Conner and me too.

She must think we're a fool for believe that lie. But it sound good. I don't think it going to happen.

Me either. I wish we can meet this man. So we can see why this girl gone nut over. Miss. Conner smile.

Yep! Me too. Maybe he have some friends. Maybe they can make us act like that.

Na, I don't that so. The both yell at the same time.

Girl, go home!

I will bring you some lunch in the morning. Well, thank you. Now I feel better.

Why?

I will be eating some of my tax money up. Miss. Low clocking out.

Now that funny.

Peter stop playing with this woman. She isn't going to keep playing this game with you. Before she slip away. Remember this game won't last forever.

Who? What talking to me? Peter look around he standing at his machine along.

What did I ate or drink for lunch? It messing with my head. I got leave that along.

Boy, what you doing? You better fire up your machine. Before the boss having you in the white house. (Office). Mr. Britt yell across the floor.

Peter shake his head. Okay! I just had a moment.

He was quiet for the rest of the day. Oh, he better get his self together. Before he be a lonely man. Mr. Britt grab a cup of water. And back to his machineFreedom, Freedom! Huh!

Why you won't allow me do my job? I don't need your help. Ma, is that your stop. The bus driver yell.

Freedom Jump up look around. Yes, Sir.

Why I'm the only one on the bus? As Freedom grabbing her things.

Ma, I guess you fell asleep. And you miss the first stop.

Okay! Thanks you have good night. Same to you ma.

Chapter 21

I got Have peace Of this

Well, let me get a bit to eat. My stomach is singing the blues. Please feed me. Penny forget she gave Paul card back. Now she do have any lunch.

Wow, my foolish self well let go into this bathroom. Say little prayer then. I will be on my fast until I get home.

As Penny walk out of the restroom a man gave her a big bag. And said enjoyed as he walk away. Little she know Paul send her some lunch.

What just happen? Her mouth drop. I smell food.

Lord, thank you answered my prayer so fast. Wow, I guess would try that again.

Some of the women behind her start whisper as walk toward the break room.

She think something she working with the boss.

Penny stop dead in her track. And turn around look at the ladies. May I help you?

No! We fine.

Okay, ladies my name is Miss. Penny. So if want talk about me because I'm the new girl. Now you know my name. As she walk in break room take her seat.

Wow, I told you about your big mouth going get yourself into trouble.

Girl, you better keep your mouth off people. Because you don't know what on their mine. And get your self-kill.

And withel they learn to be idle, wandering about from house to house; and not only idle, tattlers also and busybodies, speaking things which they ought not.

Why Lord some people just won't leave other alone? Penny whispered.

Hey, Penny you don't have eat alone come join us ladies. Okay, thanks.

My name is Mrs. Porter, Miss. Sweet peas and Miss. Green. Hello, if you need me handle some business around here. Just say the word because I need a reasoning beat some of these women around here. I know their mother sure how done it long time ago. But since she didn't that when I step up.

Penny, smile okay I keep that in mind.

Oh, I'm the nicest person up in here. But I don't like trashier women.

I know I better tip toes around here. So I can stay on her good side. She sitting over there looking a big bear. Penny whisper under her breathe.

Oh, how long been you working? Because I haven't seem you around here before. Miss. Green.

I been here just couple of week now. Okay, how you like it? So far.

Aw it okay, but right now I'm in training. Also it is a lot paperwork. And watching a lot films. Penny smile

Yep! I remember those days. I fell asleep on couple films. Girl, that dark room made me forget I was in training.

I thought was at home so I kicking off my shoes. They burst out laugh.

That until he tap me on the shoulder. I jump up wiping my mouth.

And he ask me do I need a strong coffee cup. Before he started next film. Mrs. Porter

He kind of hurt my feeling. How? Mrs. Porter

She took a bit of her sandwich.

Oh, before I leave to go home. He told me since I miss the other films. Because I stole me a nap earlier. And he say I wasn't ready take the written test yet. He also said if I don't past it the first time. I won't able take it again until next year. Because he only give it the test two time a years.

Wow, I better drink a pot of coffee. In the morning before I come in. I don't want that happen to me. I know the other day I was so sleepy. I had to stand up because I didn't want to get too comforted. I would've been like you. But I have a woman training me. Penny smiling.

That must be Mrs. Gail. She can be little grump sometimes in the morning. If don't get her some coffee in her first.

Okay, but don't take her for granted. You don't want get caught up and have to do it all over again.

Thank for the warning.

Hey, why you kick me Miss. Green?

Girl, look who walk in? Yes, I see that fine things.

Can I take him home to meet my mommy? Miss. Sweet pea whisper.

No! You will hurt him. If you think he was looking at another woman.

Hey, he coming our way. I should've check my make- up. Before I came up here. I know I don't have chance get with him.

Penny, just sat there listening to the ladies going crazy over this man.

She turn around to look who was him. It was Paul smiling.

Hello, ladies I hope you having a good day. Yes! We are.

Hey that the same man gave my training. Before they hired me Miss Porter smiling.

Okay!

I think he is the owner of this company. But I'm isn't sure you know a lot rumor around here. And you can't believe everything you hear. Miss. Porter Shaking your head.

I know right! Because I almost beat up this lady over a lie. I had her up in the air. I was getting ready slam her into the wall. Miss. Green fold her arms.

Girls, you better watch out these kind of men? Why? Miss. Porter.

I had one so fine. I was so jealous of him. He left me for another woman.

Aw, sorry hear that. Penny drop her head.

Well, that was my younger day. I won't allow that again. Penny!

Huh!

I know you have a man?

No! Not yet. I don't have time for one right now. I'm trying get this money first. I been and done that.

I hear that!

Yep! I'm isn't going to ask you have a man. Miss. Green. Why?

Because you have a quick temper. You don't mine fighting.

Well, I can't auger with that. Because I been though a lot as I was growing up. I made a promise to myself. I won't allow another man break my heart.

Keep thy heart with all diligence; for out of it are the issues of life.

Yep! I agree with her too. Penny spoke up. The bell rang.

Thanks, ladies for invite me to eat lunch with you girls. But I got go to the restroom. I think I got watch some more film too.

When I get back.

Aw, girl your welcome we enjoyed your company also. Hey, be careful of that man.

What man? Miss. Porter.

That man just came in here. Looking back at you when he left the room.

Wow, you saw something I didn't see. I don't think that man won't someone like me.

I'm isn't beautiful plus I don't have nothing offer him. As Penny cleaning off the table.

Penny, come here. Why?

Miss. Porter slap her on her cheek. Why you hit me that hurt.

I know! Because I don't want hear that anymore. You got have something offer someone. But you have love.

Why you mean? I don't understand. Penny stood there.

Let me tell you something real quick. Everyone isn't looking for things or your money. All they want someone to love them back. Things will pass always. But love will last forever.

There is no fear in love; but perfect love caseth out fear; because fear hath torment. He that fearth is not made perfect in love.

I hope you will remember that. Beside you isn't ugly. You might just put on some makeup and let someone hook up you head.

No man don't want look at the same woman. Every day the same. Every now and then fix your up different.

Oh, I didn't know I was competing for a man. Penny slower walking out the door.

Well, you matter put you name in the hat. Maybe you be the lucky one

And Girl I been put my name in it already. But I hadn't no luck yet. Miss Porter grabbing her things.

Okay, thanks I got to go. I'm late but I got use it too. Penny ran out the door and into Paul arms.

Holds on where you going? Paul look down at her. Oh, sorry going to the restroom.

Before I go back to work. I 'm kind of late.

Okay! Slow down please we can't afford you get hurt around here. We need everyone in good health.

Sorry! Again you're right my insurance haven't kick in yet. I afford a hospital bill right now. I don't want be laying up at home being bored. Penny ease around him.

Oh, wow that was a close one. Penny whisper.

Aw, I forget check on Freedom. I know she hate me by now.

I better call mom to pray for me. I'm hearing voice in my head. I know I'm isn't losing my mind.

The ring and ring.

I hope daddy don't answered the phone.

I don't want hear his mouth right now. He always want to give me a hard time. But maybe that the way he saying he miss me. Freedom holding the phone.

Hello, who is this?

Aw man, it you daddy.

What did I do now? But I hope you isn't calling to see if we cook.

Na, dad I'm isn't call about something to eat. I just need to talk to mom.

Oh, really! Yes, dad!

Excuse me my daughter.

Hey, woman! Your daughter calling you. If she ask you for some food.

You tell her she have a job stop the store. Because she never bring us nothing but hard time.

When we took care of her until she got old enough to take care of herself. That should be enough.

Give me the phone you always trying make others feel bad. That why no one don't call you anymore.

I told you woman you need to stay in your place.

Man, if don't sit your little self- down somewhere. Before I make this call. My church members love pour their holy oil out and bath you in it. You already know what happen next. They going to put their hands all over you.

Oh, woman I dare you.

Hey, hey, can you find something to do. She didn't call you. If that case she would talk to you. Instead asking for me.

Bye!

Yep! Go read your bible. Maybe the word put you to sleep. Or make you speaking in tongue. So you leave me alone.

Ooh, you make me sick sometimes.

Yep, I hope you will do every one a favor. What?

Just go ahead die. I might cry just little bit. And miss your mouth. I won't miss nothing else because the bedroom been cold in years.

Oh, mom that not nice.

Yes, I know! I just want him leave me alone sometimes.

I heard that woman. Now, you need stop playing with God. Na, I'm just speaking the truth. And you can't handle it.

Ooh, you make me sick sometimes. Daddy grab his bible walk out.

Yep! She the one need someone pray for her. God see all that hade up in her.

Mom, mom are you still there.

Oh, yes I'm sorry. You already know how your daddy he love drama.

He should've been a woman acting like that.

Mom, you know dad just bored. Since he retired he just need something to do. To make his self-feel important again.

Okay! Now I know how to handle him.

So why you calling me? I haven't heard nothing from you. I think it at least two week.

Aw, mom sorry! I been busy. I just need you pray for me. Okay! But did you pray for yourself?

Yep, but I know God haven't heard my prayer.

Girl, you like your daddy he don't any patient. Well, yep! I know that why I call you.

I know God will hear you. Well I know he probably tired of me. Because I haven't been good lately.

Okay, tell me what we praying about first.

Mom, you know I told I got a man now. But he playing game with my motion. I'm tired chase him down

What? Say that again! You doing what now? Do I need to clean my ears?

No! You heard me right mom.

I saw he in church one Sunday. So I been chasing him hoping he give me a chance. And I think he is rich too. That mean I won't have to work anymore. I be his queen and he be my king. But sometimes I see him he action like someone else.

Huh! Maybe he by polar.

Mom, please don't say that will break my heart.

You don't need me to pray for you. But you need me kick you in your behind.

Why?

Fool you don't suppose be run up behind a man. If anything it should be the other way around. He should be chase you like the dog be chasing the cat.

Aw, mom! I knew you was going to go there.

Mom, that isn't me.

I shouldn't tell you something you been hearing for years.

And the LORD God said it is not good that the man should be alone; I will make him a help meet for him.

That man job. So why you trying help.

I isn't trying let this man slip away for me. When I look up some else be smiling at me. And riding in the car I want be in.

If you have do all that to get him. When get him what going to do to keep him?

Aw, aw, mom that a good question.

But he got money I don't have to do nothing but look good for him.

Wow, I need to put hands though that phone. And chore some sense back in you. I know I didn't teach be anybody fool. That mean he going to love you.

Mom! What?

I don't need him to love me. Just long give me his bank card. Oh, my God! My daughter lost her mind. I think you right you need that prayer answered quickly. So he can bring back your brain. What the devil have stolen from you?

Mom! What?

You started acting dad now. Let get this prayer over. Before the devil get in you.

Okay! Bow you head.

Lord, I come to you asking opened my foolish daughter eyes. So she can stop running behind this man. Before she get her heart broken again. You already told us in your word. That is the man job look for us.

And you don't need no one get in your way. When it time you bring it to pass.

And it shall come to pass, if thou shalt hearken diligently unto the voice of the Lord thy God, to observe and to do all his commandment thee this, that the Lord thy God will set thee on high above all nations of earth:

Wow, mom thanks. I will talk to you later. I love you Oh, that all you wanted get a pray out me. I feel use.

Mom, I'm sorry! I didn't want you feel that way. But I got to home get ready for bible study.

You should drag dad to it too sometimes. Maybe his attitude change. You already know if die now. He going to hade and he can't take any water down there.

Yes! You have a good point there.

Yep, he need to be remind life is too short. Playing thinking he will have time to get ready.

But of the times and the seasons. Brethren, ye have no need that I write unto you

For yourselves know perfectly that the day of the Lord so cometh as a thief in the night.

The sad part about that we don't know when we going to close our eyes. Every time God allow us opened our eyes in the morning.

If confess or sins, he is faithful and just to forgive us our sins, and to cleanse us from all unrighteousness.

It another change get that thing right with him.

As it written, For thy sake we are killed all the day long; we accounted as sheep for the slaughter.

Okay, Freedom I love you too.

Aw, maybe I should call her. Aw, no I'm going to the house. And I'm find me sometimes good to eat. After I take a shower. As Peter getting ready to clock out.

The phone rang.

I hope nothing wrong with my sister.

Hey, Paul how your day going?

Well, just little busy I just came out of a business meeting. Now I going to find me sometime to eat. Paul put his hand on his stomach.

Okay, I know that feeling too. Well the reasoning I called your niece and nephew wanted to auditor. For the church Christmas play. It getting close to Christmas and they want be ready. So tonight is the last chance get play sheet. Please if that anyway you could take us put up a sheet.

Aw, man all I wanted to go home. And relax for the night. Sis. You can mess up a brother day.

Sorry!! Well, you can look them in their little face. And tell them no.

See there you always know how pull my heart string. And you already know I can't say no to them. Because we are family.

Okay, I will go. But I can't stay the hold service. I got a lot thing to do later.

Thanks! Bro.

Yes, yes let me go eat something before I go back into another meet.

I will see you later.

By that time Penny walk around the corner. Well, how everything going with you?

It okay!

What about you?

I thought I was doing okay. I until my sister call me ask would I take them to bible study tonight. So the kids get their plays sheet for the Christmas auditor. And tonight the last night to get them.

Aw, go you just might learn something.

Okay! Miss. Penny in that case you put on some clothes. Go with us then we can learn it together.

Aw, man see what done to myself. What?

I stuck my foot in my mouth. I really don't do church.

But I do need to go. So I can't keep these demon off of me around here. Penny smile.

Hey what you know about that? Paul lean against the wall. Did you forget I told I use go to the church. When I was younger.

Oh, yes you did tell me that. See I thought you was listening.

Well, I thought I did. Sometimes we can miss things. Paul holding his stomach.

Hey, what wrong with you? Why?

Chapter 22

The Big Mix up

I see you holding your stomach. Oh, I'm hungry.

I haven't eating yet. Because I just came out the meet.

Okay! I better get around this corner. Before the boss catch me. And I don't need no trouble. Well, since you talk me into it. I be ready about 6: 30 Penny start walking back toward the office.

Oh, really!

Yep!

Wow, I see you then and you can meet my sister also. With her bad kids.

Little Penny know Paul go to the same church. Freedom also go too.

The phone rang.

Hello, Miss. Penny! How are you?

I been okay just busy with all this training. Okay!

Sorry, I haven't call you. Hey I do miss hanging out with you. Awa, you do?

Yep! You haven't tell me about that man of yours. When I'm going to meet the prince.

Well, I hoping soon. But he isn't a prince yet. I haven't kiss yet turn him back.

Okay, you still got that since of human. Yep! That isn't going to change.

Hey, I talk you later after I get off work. I got pay these bills. Okay, but I maybe at bible study tonight.

Wow! I see someone getting deep up in church.

Aw, I don't know all about that. But if I go every now and then. I just may learn something. Maybe I could hook you up.

No, I'm good.

Freedom shaking her head. This girl don't have a clue. What I'm talking about.

I told you I'm isn't looking for a man. Penny stood in the hall. No, silly I'm talking about Jesus.

Oh, yes I can use a lot of that. Maybe my life change for the good. Then I might be able caught me a godly man.

''But be countinually with a godly man, whom thou knowest to keep the commandments of the Lord,

Whose, mind is according to thy mind, and will sorrow with thee, if thou shalt miscarry.

Okay! Yep right. Girl, I got to go now.

Okay, me too. I'm still at work too. Freedom walked fast to her machine.

Girl, you better care before you going to need your man find you another job. Miss. Conner yell to her.

Freedom shaking her head. Na, that give more reasoning to stay home.

Okay, don't be a fool thinking you can't depend on other. They can mess you up. If you isn't prepared.

That what happen me my baby daddy left me. I thought he was going take care us for the rest of our life. I had to do things. I'm isn't proud of it. I had to find a way out of that lifestyle I got myself into. Trying feed my babies. Tears roll down her face.

Thy tongue devisth mischiefs; like a sharp razor, working deceitfully.

Thanks for the warning. Freedom throw her hand in the air wave at her.

This girl don't get it. I guess it got slap her beside her head. Maybe she will stop dreaming.

Pride goeth before destruction, and an haughty spirit before a fall.

Well, me let get this day over with.

Mom, said if you find a fool. Let them bump their own head. Just maybe they will come to their senses. Miss. Conner whisper to herself.

Peter run to the clock knowing that voice was still messing with him.

Hey, Peter are you alright? Is this place on fire?

No I'm alright! I think I eat or drink something messing my head. So I'm going home jump in the shower. And lay down maybe I feel better.

Well, okay at least this isn't on fire. I'm too old running up out here. Plus thanks God for this. My kids in school. And they have a part time job. But they still begging me for some bread. I wish I had read the fine print of having kids. What require of and how much they going cost me. Or is one job be enough support them.

I wish someone told me I got keep them for life time. I would have run the other ways.

But if any provide not his own, and specially for those of his own house, he hath denied the faith, and is worse than an infidel.

Well, yes thanks for the advice. Now you got me thinking do I want kids? If you going through so much trouble with them. Do I want be like you Mr. Britt.

No, I probably be in jail for what they call children abuse. But my mother call it a beating. So this child's won't be thinking they can take of over. I have them run around sacred of me.

He that spareth his rod hateth his son: but he that loveth him chasteneth him betimes.

Yes, I know I been there before with my second daughter. Thinking she can sneak out the house go see this boy.

The first time got me. When I found what she doing. I set a trap for her.

How? As they was walking out the door.

Oh, I put some firecracker outside her window. I heard her one night pretend she going the bathroom.

So I ease out to the side door with my lighter in my hand. I got a chair sat behind tree. So she wouldn't see me. I waited and waited on her finally ease out the window. I allow her a few minute got herself together. Finally the boy walk up and started kissing all over her.

I politely wait for a while see what next he going to try next. When I see he was going too far. And she trying to stop him. Boy, I had fire in my eyes. Ready go to jail this night. Because I'm about whip these kids behind. But I little voice back of my little head. Said isn't worth it.

You already know what happen next.

No! Please tell me. They standing in the parking a lot.

I fire up those firecracker it went off sounding like gun shooting. They thought I was shooting at them. They was hollowing and screaming. The boy yell please don't kill me. He ran so fast you would thought he was the road runner on the cartoon show. My neighbors ran outside. And someone call the police on me.

When they got there I made my daughter explain what was going on. And all her friends peeking out the window. And she still mad at for that.

Boy, you just made my day. Peter can't stop laughing. Alright Mr. Britt go home get some rest. I will see you in the morning. Peter got in the car.

He finally got home getting ready take a shower. The phone ring.

This must be Freedom call me back. That what he thought.

Hey, baby i just got home from work. I was about to call you. Yes, darling you was?

What?

You isn't Freedom.

No, I hope not. You know I don't get down like that. Doug stop playing game with me.

Na, that sound like you.

So who this Freedom? You will call her back?

Oh, a little girl I ran into at church.

What? Boy you said you going to church find you a woman. I thought you was joking.

Why? I told you. I'm tired be alone.

Yes, I can see that. I'm beginning feel the same.

Well, when I get back in town in a couple month. You can fill me in.

What? I thought you going be gone for a year.

Na, my parents getting on my nerves. It time me bounce (leave) out of here. I can't take it anymore. They still trying treat me like a child. I'm grow up now.

When I was a child, I spake as a child, I understood as a child, I thought as a child: but when I became a man, I put away childish things.

Oh, maybe they feeling guilt what they didn't do. When you was a child. And trying make it up to you.

Repent therefore of this thy wickedness, and pray God, if perhaps the thought of thine heart may be forgiven thee.

Maybe so! I'm isn't trying hear that right now. I been forgive them. I wish they will let it go.

Forbearing one another, and forgiving one another, if any man have a quarrel against any: even as Christ forgave you, so also do ye.

Okay!

So how my house and car?

Oh, we doing great. I just hate leave it. Peter started laugh. Maybe someday you can the same.

Yep, I think I will too. I kind of like come home and I can enjoyed it.

Hey, your girl got money right? Man, why you ask me that for?

Well, do she or not.

I don't know yet. It too early to tell. We haven't dating long. I'm still working on it. But I know one thing about her.

What?

She love going to church.

Well, in your case that a good thing. What you mean?

At least she love the Lord or pretending. Trying make you feel like she is a good girl.

Doug! What?

Shout up? You don't know what you talk about. Well, what you going to do with her?

Now there you go again.

What? I'm just asking a simple question. Is something wrong with that?

Well, no depend the way you look at it.

Aw, I think will keep seeing her. And try find out more about her. Before I kick her to the curve.

Hey you mean before she kick you to the curve. I bet you still pretend you got going on. That how you got her. Right you don't have answered it.

Man, you can mess up good dream. Yep, I think so too.

She look at the way I was dressing. And the car I was driving.

Boy, you got find out if she a gold dipped. All about the money. Or she looking a nice guy who would love her.

If she all about the money you already lost her. But if she not you just might have a chance.

Yep, you make good point there.

Well, you don't have long. You can't pretend you me. I think I want my life back. Doug smile

Yes, I figure you would. But I didn't think it would be this soon. Peter thinking.

Sorry, things happen. I hope you learn something by been rich. Now you know isn't so fun after all. Because you have money don't make you happy.

Sometimes it can give you a head ack. If you don't trust the people around you. And it going to been hard love a woman. All you think she want your money.

Oh yes it would for me. I never had it like this before.

It kind of feel good. Waking up in a big house. And eat whatever you want. Driving any car. Plus you can almost get any woman you want.

Yep, that maybe is true. But it get old you just want be in peace sometimes. So you can think and relax.

Maybe have a good point too. If I stop look at my situation. I'm in peace and I can go to my little home to relax.

Now you beginning see the clear picture. Sometime I wish I had a simple life. No more head ark because I got to make a big decision. In the blink of an eyes I can lose it all. Then I be homeless.

Wow, I didn't see it that way. Doug. Sorry! I was been jealous of you.

No, don't be you have that right. Because you haven't been in my shoes

In that case I was envy of you. What? I can't believe that.

Yep! That the truth.

Wow, you going make me have tears in my eyes. Okay, okay don't do that.

Well, Peter I got go finished up something before I come home. Okay, thanks again giving me the opportunity been you.

Yep, yep! You have a good night. I hope I will met this girl of yours. Maybe she have a friend for me. When get back in town. I don't know. But we can find out.

Okay! I love you my brother.

Wow, this game isn't going to last forever. I got to figure my next move.

Lord, I got come clean. Please show me out to get of this jam. But I do kind of like her.

I know she don't want avenge man. I'm just barely my paying bills. Nor I don't have big house or a nice car. Peter prayed.

Little he know God already putting things in place for the both.

Why I got to fool with my sister tonight? I want go home relax it been a long day. Paul whispered as he come out of the board meeting. But I promise so let me get myself together. Then again it may okay since I talk Penny in go with me.

Again why I put my foot in my mouth for. Knowing I don't do church more. Freedom fool me once.

She had me up in a funeral someone I didn't know. I still sometime have nightmare. Looking down at them and they are smiling at me. I know they thinking why this woman at my funeral. She don't know me. But she kind of cute though

Boy, I can't wait get this day over with. So I can run home take nap before I go to bible study tonight.

It would look bad If I fall asleep up in there. And miss the hold thing. Plus I never know Peter may change his mind drop by the church. So I better keep my eyes opened. Plus never know I may have run up out of there.

My brother really do need find his a good girl. So she can help him spend some of his money. I know he need a long vacation from work.

Oh, maybe I need to hook him up with my old friend.

Na, that won't work they younger. They act to childish. And they probably mess up his head take all his money. And high and dry. Okay, let put my little head together. While a minute let call me Gail so can snoop around. Maybe she can help me put thing together. I hope this new girl he went the interview isn't married or got a man.

Maybe something can spark between them.

All I have to do throw a little dinner together with Gail help. At least I can do that for him. He deserve it because always take care of me. So why not return the favor.

Little Sis know Paul already got his eyes on Penny.

The bell rang.

I see you girls later.

I'm tired my feet hurt all want to do relax. Before Paul pick me up for bible study. Penny whisper as she going out the door.

Hey, Miss. Penny may I see before you clock out. Please come in my office.

Everybody looking at her whisper to one another.

Well, he is my boss call me. Wow I must be famous or something. I see y'all women jealous of me. But I can't help that. Penny thought to herself ask walked toward Paul.

Yes!

Oh I'm sorry for calling you out like that. It okay!

I wanted remind you about tonight.

Oh I haven't forgot. I'm kind of in a hurry. I need caught this bus. Before it leave me.

Okay, but I can take you home if you like. Paul smile Oh no, brother not today. Thank anyway.

Why?

Just peek out your window you know all those women out there have a crush on you. Plus I'm the new girl on the block. They think I'm trying move in on their piece of meat.

Yep, right Paul started laughing.

See you trying get me beat up. I can't be having a path over my eyes. I barely see with two eyes.

I think I take my chance on the bus. Well you can pick me up for work in the morning. It begin getting cold out there on the bus stop. And I can't afford get sick. Somebody got paid these bills up in my house. I'm taking any volunteer Penny stood at the door smiling.

Girl, go home!

Okay then. I respect that. I see you tonight.

Yep! I be ready. Penny smile.

Freedom finally made it home.

I better find my clothes for tonight. Before I take a nap. I don't want to be rushing at the last minute.

I got get this picture. Somehow of this man. Just maybe I can have peace on the job. I hope he surprise me and show up. So I can steal his picture.

I hope my sister be ready when I pull up in the driveway. I don't won't wait 30 minute.

It usually take her and the kids get ready. I'm ready get this night over.

So I can enjoyed my bed. It just might be a late morning for me. It depend how I roll out the bed.

Penny finally got home. Let kick off these shoes they been hurting foot all day. I matter well put them in the trashes. Because I'll never going to wear them anymore. When this girl get paid I got go shopping.

Now since I'm working in the law firm. I get look good just like the others ladies. Penny thinking to herself.

I better get out here before I get caught up in that ugly traffic. Some of these people can't driver either. I have a big night ahead. I have two beautiful women going be on my side too. Well, Sis will meet Penny for the first time. And I hope she don't make her feel bad.

Because she is over protected of me. That won't be good on my behalf.

Maybe I need talk to her. Let her know I'm working on getting a date with her. Please don't mess up things for me. Paul thinking to his self. As grabbing his things

I got get into this closet to find something to wear for tonight.

Oh, now I know I'm wearing my black and red dress. I and Penny bought it last years. For Apostle Gary birthday party. The guys couldn't keep their eyes off of us. Freedom run to the closet.

Penny shaking her head I don't know what I'm wearing. I don't want under or over dress.

Let me look in my closet pray I find something. The first thing she saw it was the dress her and Freedom wore to the Apostle Gary birthday party.

Wow, Lord this must my sign. I'm wearing this dress maybe I all the eyes be on me. Na, I'm isn't trying be hook up with these old men there.

Little the both going to find out they both wearing the same dress.

Boy, I don't have long to break the news to Freedom.

That I'm isn't rich. Mr. Britt was right I should've been honest from the beginning. I know she going to run the others way. Oh, I know what to do I will surprise her by coming to church tonight. Maybe I can talk to her after the service. Peter toss and turn thinking. Then he jump up and ran into the shower. Throw some clothes on and grab his bible. Rushing out the door.

Well, let grab me something to eat. Before Paul pull up in the driveway. I don't want my stomach singing the blues. While we are driving down the road. Penny wash her hands.

I need hurry up get dress before I miss this bus. Then I will be home tonight. Freedom run into the bathroom. Boy, it would nice Peter be there waiting for me.

Na! That isn't going to happen. Let me stop dreaming.

Lord, why I can't figure out this man? I know he got bank. But he playing these game.

As Freedom putting her hi. She heard a soft voice. Don't let your little eyes deceive you. She jump up look around the room. She stood there alone.

But be ye doers of the word, and not hearers only, deceiving your own selves.

I know I better hurry up get out of this house. Get some Jesus up in me. I'm been hearing these voices lately. I can't tell no one they will think I'm gone crazy.

So I'm going to ease over to the kitchen table grab my holy oil sprinkle all round my house. I hope when I come back house the voices be gone. Freedom grab her coat and run down to the bus stop.

I don't feel right. Something isn't right. But I can't figure this out at the moment.

Little she know Paul & Freedom going to the same church.

Paul finally made it home. I better call Sis let know please ready when I blow my horn. I don't feel like sit in the car for thirty minute. And I got drive cross town too.

Hey, kids we got get ready uncle Paul be here soon. He just call me.

Okay, mom! I'm put on my shoes. And I'm look for my coat.

Wow! Who big beautiful house? Oh, this sister house.

Okay! She must got big bank (money). You say what?

Oh, sorry!

She must have money.

Na, mom and daddy give her that house. They got tried her with those bad kids. So they move out.

Paul, stop lying.

Your parents just move out. Penny smiling. Yep! They did.

Great!

Hey, come in! I give you a tour real quick. Paul open her door.

First let me see if they really.

Okay! Great I don't mind wish on a star. What you mean?

Oh, I know it take me a year or two of my pay check. Just pay the light bill.

Paul, burst out laughing. Why you laughing?

What you say? Girl, you never know what God have for you. That true Penny smile. But I don't won't a house like this one. Who going to clean it up. All that dust and spider web.

Trust in the Lord, and do good; so shalt thou dwell in the land, and verily thou shalt be fed.

Delight thyself also in the Lord; and he shall give thee the desires of thine heart.

Oh, really!

Yep! Just like that. But one thing you must do first. Yes! I know I need to repent. Penny

Commit thy way unto the Lord; trust also in him; and shall bring it to pass.

Well, I'm can't argue with that.

But I was trying to say. You must believe that it is so.

And Jesus said unto them, I am the bread of life: he that cometh to me shall never hunger; and he that believeth on me shall never thirst.

Oh, you going to put the word on me.

Of courage that how play. Paul knock on the door. Well, Mr. I'm going to let that go.

Sorry! But we can't beat God giving.

Little Penny know she about to move in a big house. Hey, Sis this is my co- worker Miss. Penny.

Wow! Bro. she is beautiful. Where you find her?

She need a job and we need someone do the work. So everything working out for the good.

Oh, I'm! Penny smile.

Paul, I think I'm going to like this one. Wait a minute! Can I say something?

No! The both girl yell. Leave her alone.

Wow, you two trying double team me. Paul smile Yep! I love have someone on myself. Penny smiling. Great! My Bro. can be boring sometimes.

Hey, no fair! I can't argue with you. Hey, Uncle who is this?

Oh, she my co- worker.

Na, uncle stop trying fool us. She going to be our auntie soon. Paul and Penny look at each other.

Penny, smile I don't know about that.

Paul couldn't believe what your nephew said.

Well, they just prophecy to you two. Sis. Smile looking over at Paul.

Hey, give Miss. Penny let me give a quick tour. Then we got go. Okay!

First let me help you find your bible. Sis

Paul, put his over her mouth Bro what wrong with you?

You lose your mind.

No! I don't want you spoil it for me. So please don't tell her I'm rich.

Okay! But what you got yourself into now?

Girl, I will tell you later. Just keep your big mouth closed for me.

Okay? Bro. I want the full detail.

I will! Thanks you. I owe you one. Yep, yep!

Miss. Penny let me show you this too big house. But I can't argue because my parents give to me. They didn't see me homeless.

Okay!

Please excuse it haven't been clean today. I got find me a maiden. So they can hook this house up.

Oh, wait a minute! I hope you isn't too cheap like your brother. You won't find a maiden.

Oh, really!

Yep! But if you give up some cash. Maybe you already find one. You mean you don't mine come up in here clean up my house. Yes, I can use that extra change. I can do it on the weekend.

Okay, done deal. Paul!

What?

Where you found this rare diamond? I think you need keep her around.

What you are talking? She just my co- worker. Yep, right? Sis yell.

Now you sound like the kids.

Sorry! But I can't help myself. I'm falling in love with her spirit. Wow! You don't sound like my sister. I use to know. Paul smiling.

Well, is that a good thing?

Yes, I still got to love you.

Penny, gave her a big hug. With tear in her eyes. Why you cry?

No one never make me feel love like this. Yep, I be your sister from another mother. The both burst out laughing.

Girl, just enjoyed the moment. Thank you.

Why? What did I do? Penny smile.

You have my brother face lite up. I haven't seen him like that in a long time.

Oh, really! Yep!

I'm just been myself. This me whatever you see me seven day of the week.

I don't change for no one. It too much hassle. Soon or late you can't hide forever.

Well, you have a good point. I try that but still my baby daddy still left me. But thank God for my brother step in when he did. I didn't know what I was going to do. Because I started depend on him to make me happy.

Girl, don't feel bad. I been there too. I had to learn if you want to be happy. You better do it yourself. Man will fall you.

It is better trust the Lord than to put confidence in man. Blessed are ye that hunger now: for ye shall be filled. Blessed are ye that weep now: for ye shall laugh.

Yep! Let go to church. And get some Jesus up in us. Well, let see! Penny look up at her.

What you ladies smiling about? Paul closing the door. Bro. It a girl thing! You wouldn't understand.

Okay, miss. Penny what did you do to my sister? Nothing, why?

Because I haven't seen her smiling and laughing like this in a long time.

Oh, is this a bad thing. Penny look over at him.

No, it great see her smiling. It something about you I like. What?

I guess your beauty spirit. Aw, thank.

Girl, you better accept it. This man really don't give to many people compliment.

Oh, really! Yep!

Sis you know that isn't true. As Paul pull up in the church parking a lot.

Hey, wait a minute you go to the same church my friend Freedom.

Okay! I hope that good thing.

Well, I don't know about that. Because she bought me here looking for a man. But it was a funeral.

What? They burst out laughing. Hey, was he dead?

Now Paul you trying be funny.

No, I don't know. I didn't check to see if he was dead or sleep. I was so mad when I found out what she done to me. I tried hurry up leave. But the ushers made me stay to the end.

Wow! Why you didn't sing a sole while you there.

You still have joking. Oh, now I owe you for calling me out. I'm sorry! But I can't help myself. I haven't a laugh like this in a long time.

Girl, believe me he isn't lying. Sis smile.

Well, I will let you have this fun now. You better watch your back. I will found something on you.

When I start joking with you. Just take it like a man.

Paul started get quite.

I got you! It was great see a big man humble yourself. Penny smile.

Well, you guys let get out this car. So we can find a good seat. While I'm here I matter will listening to the word.

Uncle Paul! Huh!

Why you isn't holding our new auntie hand?

Oh, no! We just co- worker. He looking speechless. Why you don't love her? Kids smiling.

Boy, your mom need stop you two watching too much television after dark.

Penny, couldn't believe what they was saying.

Listening to what come out a babe mouth. Sis. Smile sorry I didn't teach them that.

And said unto him, Hearest thou what these say? And Jesus saith unto them, Yea; have ye never read, Out of the mouth of babe and suckling thou hast perfected praise?

It okay! They just kids curious. Penny shake her head.

Paul whispered over to Penny wow these kids got a sense of human.

Yep! They do!

Well, it good thing my sister think you be good for me. Oh, what that mean? Penny look up at him.

I forgot tell about that. So if anyone got use the restroom. It a good time go. Before the crowd come in. Paul whispered.

Okay, I know that right. I haven't forget how the usher made me wait. Penny hurry look for the restroom.

I hope this bus hurry up it getting cold out here. That why I got see what up with this man. So I won't have to be out here. I can be in a warm car. Freedom whispered to herself.

Maybe I need go down to the church hope I can catch Freedom. And be straight up with her. I'm isn't rich but I'm will work hard to make her happy.

Yep, I better get it together. And take my friends advice before I lose her. Peter ran into the shower. And grab some clothes from the closet.

Little he know he and Paul going to have the same outfit on.

Thanks God the bus finally here. I hope I'm isn't too late find a good seat. Boy, I know I need a good word tonight. Plus I need the Pastor pray for me. Before I lose my mind fooling with this man.

Again I say unto you, That if two of you shall agree on earth as toughing anything that they shall ask, it shall be done for them of my Father which is in heaven.

As Freedom get off the bus.

Boy, I got go. I don't want be late. Having the people turning around look at me. That make me feel funny. Peter jump in the car spin off.

Hey, I think I find some good seat. They isn't to close the front nor the back. Paul smiling.

Okay, we'll sit here. But can I sit close to the door. Penny ask. Yes!

Thanks! I just might have run up out here.

Yep! That maybe a good idea. It just maybe another funeral tonight. Paul whisper and smiling.

Oh, I wish I had a cold glass water right about now. Why?

I cool you off. You trying be funny again. I think you better as the Pastor lay hand on you.

Before I do it to you. Have you be speaking in tongue. Penny pat him on his kneel.

Okay, sorry!

Me too! She shake head up.

See mommy look over at them they acting a kid. I thought I that was my job. Since they already doing my job. I think I be good for a change.

Sis. Burst out of laughing.

What wrong with you? Paul got quite. Sorry! It wasn't nothing.

I better got up in here find me a good seat. Oh, I got use the restroom before I go in. Freedom trying caught her breathe running up the stairs.

Peter just pull up in the parking a lot.

Wow, it a lot people here tonight. I hope Freedom didn't change her mind stay home. If so I will stay to the end of the service.

Maybe I will learn something. While I'm here. Peter locking the door.

Boy, now I got use the restroom.

Uncle why didn't go before we sat down. Sorry, I got help myself.

You need stop drinking so much water. Knowing we coming to church. It will make you use it too. That why mom don't allow me no water. Before I go the bed. I just might use it .

Paul couldn't say anything. Because he is right.

Hurry back the service about to start. And the usher going to escort you back to your like child.

Well, I back soon this church isn't small now.

By time Peter walk in take a seat close the back door. But he just miss Freedom going to the restroom.

But instead she met Paul in the hall.

Hey, Peter I'm glad you made it. I thought you had something to do.

Paul keep walking to the restroom.

I wondered why he didn't answered me. I know heard me. Freedom shake her head. Should I stand by the bathroom? Or wait until him walking down the hall.

Why this woman walking behind me call me Peter?

She must think I'm have a twin brother. Or she lost he mind. Mom! Huh, baby.

Why uncle sitting by the door.

I don't know? Maybe he forgot where we are sitting. Go tell him where we are sitting.

Hey go, tell your uncle we're sitting down there.

Hey uncle, let me grab his hand and pull him out his seat. Pointed over to mom and Penny.

Wow, who is this little boy? Peter confuse and he can't speak Paul did you get lost coming from the restroom?

No, I haven't been to the restroom. I just came in take me a seat. Okay, but why she keep call me Paul.

By that time an usher yell please turn off your cell. If your phone ring it better Jesus calling you home.

The hold church burst out laughing.

Well, I better turn my off. I'm isn't ready go yet. I have unfinished things to do. I need more time. Penny whisper over to Peter. He look at her with a funny look on his face.

Sorry, I was just joking. Okay!

Wow! Why Paul acting funny with me now? I thought everything going well with us.

Why, this woman keep calling me Paul? And the other beautiful woman smiling at me. I wish I met her first.

I hope this woman find that man name Peter. So I can get back to my seat. And I hope I can catch the prayer.

I need it been a long day at work. Plus my sister got me here. I might well try let the spirit come in. As Paul walking out the restroom.

About time I catch you. Paul, look around.

Who?

You? Freedom grab his hand.

You can't run from me now. I'm tried! I been running behind you for months. After church I need you give me an answered? If we going to call this a relationship. Or you going to keep playing this game.

Paul, was in shock. He was speechless.

This woman is nut. I got find away from her. Lord, what I'm going to do?

Hey, I think I heard someone calling my name. So I better go see who looking for me. Paul hoping she will fall for that.

Na, they can wait until I finished with you.

So don't worry be happy. I'm so tried telling my co- worker asking do I have a man.

And they don't believe me unless I show them a picture of us together.

Okay, let me find someone take it. Paul hoping he can escape for Freedom.

Na, we wait after church. So let grab some good seat. Freedom grab his hand.

What I got myself into. I just wanted use the restroom. It must be a trick. So I going play alone with her. Oh, I know will do. I hope they haven't said the pray yet. When she close her eyes. Then I'm dip(leave) too.

Peter I got find Freedom and let know the truth Lord. And I hope she don't run the other way. So I got find away from these people.

I know I tell them I got use the restroom. Peter thinking to his self.

Hey, I'm be back.

Where you going now? The service about to started. Penny whisper.

I'm going to the little boy room.

I thought you just came from it. Because told us we need to go before the service started.

Oh, I did?

Yep! Paul you already? You isn't like the Paul know couple our ago.

Sorry, I can't help myself but duty call. I think I ate something early isn't agreeing with my stomach.

Okay, do you need your nephew go with you? So you won't get lost again.

Oh, I think I can manner. Peter hold his stomach pretending it hurting.

Well, okay you don't have long before they start praying. I would like us pray together. Now I call you my family.

Wow! I'll trying.

Hey, Sis. Huh!

Your brother don't seem like his self.

What you mean?

I don't know but I feel like is a difference person.

Oh, maybe he just tired and get grump because sleep may caught up with. Sis whispered over to her.

Okay, maybe you right.

Let everything please turn off your cell phone please. And stand for pray and the reading of the word.

Now, it time to make my move.

Freedom close her eyes and reach other to grab Paul hand. But Paul headed to the restroom to hide out. Until they deacon stop praying. So can find Penny.

But they both walk by each other. Peter and Paul. Didn't notice each other.

While a minute the both stop at the same time. This can't be me they both say it at the same time. I must be losing my mind up in here.

I got run up out of here. Maybe I slip into a dream or something. But end up in the restroom. And run to the sink washing their face. Hoping this nightmare go away.

I know,i must got this preacher lay his hand on me. Got this demon out of me. The both thought the same.

Paul left the restroom one way. And Peter went the other way. They both end up where they belong.

Hey, uncle are you okay? Yes, I'm fine.

Okay, why you going to the restroom so much? Now the rude because doing to much walking.

Oh, wait a minute! Sis what nephew talking about?

I don't understand? I haven't been to the restroom once tonight.

I may have to go after church. Paul had a funny look on his face. Sis and Penny look at each other.

Wow! I think you're right Penny. What?

Nothing! Sis whispered.

Brother I think you need some prayer? Yes, I can you use some of that too.

Peter look around spotted Freedom. I'm glad to see.

Okay, but why you left middle of pray? I tried to hold your hand. Oh, you did! Peter shaking head. I think this woman losing her mind too. Maybe I should leave this one a lone. Before the demon rise up out of her. Peter thinking to his self. Also did you thought about what I ask you early.

Oh, what you mean? He had a lost look on his face. He pulse for a second trying get his thought together. Okay, you play the silence game. Huh!

By that time he about to answered her. The usher walk by put her hand over her mouth.

Now, I got wait after church maybe he be honest with me the truth.

Oh, wow! Now I know need this prayer. Or a strong drink to clam my nerves down.

Well, thirty minute has pass finally the preacher ask alter call. And if anyone need somebody for with them.

Peter and Paul jump up at the same time. I got to get in this line. Okay! I will go with you. I need some of that too. Penny grab Paul hand.

I told you mom Uncle find him a girlfriend.

Boy, be quiet. You are too much. Sis just smiling maybe you right son.

What you doing? Freedom has a surpise look on own face. I'm going to get some of this prayer. Peter stand up.

Oh, no you isn't going to leave me alone. I'm going too. Freedom grab his hand.

Wow, I finally got the man of my dream. I wish my co- worker can see me now.

They all walk down the crowded asle. But still didn't noticed each other.

The preacher shake his head. He couldn't believe what he was seeing. He whispered over to another Preacher.

Please hurry go to my office look in my desk it two letter Peter and Paul name on it.

okay! Thank!

The Preacher wave his hand telling them come up front. They turn around look in each other face. This can't be truth.

This must be trick or something. Peter and Paul just stood there in shock.

Hey, wait minute! Oh my god this you freedom. Yep! Penny.

The both in shock standing there.

Someone please tell me what going here. This must a joking someone playing on me. Freedom yelling.

She forgot she was in the church. Everyone just frozen.

Peter and Paul please come closer. I can explain your my mother prayer been answered.

The two look at each other puzzled.

Yes, I know you probably think you two that in the move call the twilight zone.

Your birth mother was sick after she have you two. And she came to me for help. To see if he can find a nice couple. Who couldn't have kids. And be grateful adopted two little baby. I try my best keep you together. But no one wanted too. Either they accept one of you. Or you have be put in a foster care. But couldn't allow it. Because I promise your mother. I put you a loving home. So had to separate you two. Knowing I know I did the right now. And look at you all these years I been praying you two find one another. God my prayer.

They both down in tears.

I know something wasn't complete in my life. Paul smile.

Yes, I know I felt the same brother.

They crying and hugging each other. They couldn't beilve they was twin.

Wow, that explained why they was acting funny. Now, Penny why you up in here?

This is another funeral. Freedom laugh.

You trying been funny. No, this is my co worker. Who actually training me on the job. And he talk me into come to church with him and his sister.

Wait a minute! That who I saw with some kids. I was at the bus stop one night.

Yep!

Okay, that mean Peter was telling the truth. I guess!

And I must run into Peter at grocery store one night. Thinking it was Paul. Huh!

Freedom still going to be shock when she find Peter isn't rich. It was all for a show.

But on the other hand Paul going come clean. He is the owner of the law firm. And he want to put her house on the big hill. With the white picker fence.

Ladies please allow us men do our job. Because you out of order. According to the bible. That our job as man pursue you. In Proverbs 18: 22 I'm using King James Version. Who findeth a wife findeth a good thing, and obtaineth favour of the Lord, Also wives , submit yourselves unto your own husband, as unto the Lord.

In the meanwhile wait on the Lord. Submit yourselves to Lord. And said Psalm 37: 4-5 Delight thyself also in the Lord: and shall give thee the desires of thine heart.

Commit thy way unto the Lord: trust also in him; and he shall bring it to pass.

Please look these book coming soon to your near book store and online.

That man of mine
Mom you must be crazy
Caught up in the moment T
o my father

Too young too soon a
They just my roommate aa
It's a twist mess
When a man find a wife aa
A lie can hurt
Because of you
You better get that thing right

www.ingramcontent.com/pod-product-compliance
Lightning Source LLC
Chambersburg PA
CBHW050331160726
48002CB00001B/271